INSTRUCTIONS FOR THE SOUL

Also by Annie and Byron Kirkwood:

Mary's Message of Hope (Annie Kirkwood)
Mary's Message to the World (Annie Kirkwood)
Messages to Our Family (Annie & Byron Kirkwood)
Survival Guide for the New Millennium (Byron Kirkwood)

INSTRUCTIONS
FOR THE
Soul

Prayers, Affirmations, and Meditations
for Daily Living
as compiled from *Messages to Our Family*

ANNIE AND BYRON KIRKWOOD

Blue Dolphin Publishing

Blue Dolphin Publishing, Inc.
P.O. Box 8, Nevada City, CA 95959
Orders: 1-800-643-0765

ISBN: 0-931892-34-1

Library of Congress Cataloguing-in-Publication Data

Kirkwood, Annie, 1937–
    Instructions for the soul : prayers, affirmations, and
meditations for daily living as compiled from Messages to
our family / Annie and Byron Kirkwood.
        p.   cm.
    ISBN 0-931892-34-1 (pbk.)
    1. Spirit writings.   2. Prayer—Miscellanea.
3. Meditation—Miscellanea.   I. Kirkwood, Byron.
II. Kirkwood, Annie, 1937– Messages to our family.
III. Title.
BF1301.K558 1996
133.9'3—dc20   96-30462
                                                CIP

Cover design: Lito Castro

Printed in the United States of America by
Blue Dolphin Press, Grass Valley, California

9   8   7   6   5   4   3   2

CONTENTS

PREFACE

After the book, *Messages to our Family* was released, my husband and I began to hear from people who were reading the book. Many requested that the lessons on prayer and the affirmations be published in a separate book. Our publisher, Blue Dolphin Publishing, was receiving similar requests. This book is a result of those requests. Contained within are the lessons about prayer and meditation. I feel that they go hand-in-hand and need to be together. Also you will find some questions and other information I use in my seminars and workshops.

I use personal experiences and insights throughout my part of the book. This doesn't in any way mean that I have the "right" way of approaching this material. Nor does it indicate that I consider myself an expert. Since I don't have an extensive educational background, all I have are my experiences and thoughts to share. Please accept these experiences, thoughts, and insights as my way of encouraging you to find your own way to use the material.

In 1986 I began a search for the "really, really, real, real truth." In a bookstore I found a book that literally fell off the bookshelf, not once, but three times. With the encouragement of the clerk at the store, I bought the book and read it until the wee hours of the night. The book I was so engrossed in was *The God-Mind Connection* (Team-Up, 1987) by Jean K. Foster. In this book, which were communications that Jean had with the Brotherhood of God, I found a way to contact a source for information. Toward the back of the book, the Brotherhood gave instructions for setting up your own contact with them. I followed the directions and began the most incredible communication of my life.

Certainly I had many doubts and misgivings, because I couldn't believe I had made contact. I wasn't the kind of person that could follow directions and have success. For me, even following the directions on a cake box didn't bring the desired results with ease. So I doubted and questioned if this was really coming through me, or was I just mouthing platitudes and pretty sayings. With my husband's encouragement, I called Jean and read a part of one of the messages that I had received. She felt confident that what I had read was consistent with her impressions of the Brotherhood. She verified that indeed I had made contact.

Every morning I set aside a time to meditate, pray, and see if I could, or would, receive any messages. Every day without fail, the most wonderful and enlightening words flowed easily through my mind. I took them down on a computer and kept copies of my daily messages. When my husband, Byron, came home from work, he eagerly read what had been received. One day a question he had asked in his mind was answered. I was quite perplexed when the words I heard said, "Tell Byron . . ." and what came through didn't make any sense to me. When he read it, he said, "This is the answer to a question I'd asked in my mind and didn't tell you about." We were both quite happy since our questions were being answered, and we were being encouraged daily in gentle and loving ways to seek God.

Several months later I received a request from Mary, Mother of Jesus, to take her words down and send them out to the world. I debated with Mary, pointing out that I wasn't Catholic and thought she had made a huge mistake by contacting me. I didn't think anyone would believe me, and I was afraid. At that time of my life I was living in fear and terror. I'd realized that I was suffering from agoraphobia and was keeping it a secret. I used bluster and gave the outer appearance of being able to handle anything, when in reality I was afraid to go out the door.

Finally, with the encouragement of my husband, I agreed to take down Her words as long as I could remain anonymous. For two years I took down this message, and it became the book, *Mary's Message to the World.* It's been translated into ten languages: English, both an American version and a British, German, French, Spanish, Portuguese, Italian, Icelandic, Greek, Japanese, and recently, Russian. Mother Mary's message is definitely reaching the world just as She requested. But it had nothing to do with me except that I worked as Her stenographer and simply took down the words that poured into my mind each day. At the time of publishing this book, I consented to use my name because of the encouragement of Mother Mary, my husband, publisher, and editors.

Every morning after I had received my message from Mary, the Brotherhood would give me words of encouragement, suggestions, and new insights. Daily, Mary urged me to pray. She asked that I meditate. I increased my prayer time and my meditations. Yet each day, another request was made to pray more and to meditate more. I was spending several hours in prayer and meditation.

After a few months of receiving messages from Mary and the Brotherhood, both requested that we gather our children. We were told they would be taught all the wonderful things we were learning.

We asked our children. One of our sons didn't think he should come, even though all the others had accepted. At that time he was an active alcoholic. He let me know that he was "a big boy and didn't go anywhere without his beer." I assured him I wanted him to join us. He was still reluctant and said he didn't think "they," meaning Mother Mary and the Brotherhood, wanted him there under those conditions. I asked Mother Mary about his reluctance to attend. I was told to allow him to come any way he wanted to, and with anything he chose to bring with him. Mary said, "Let him come any way he wants and bring whatever he chooses. Do not make any comment with your voice or face." I was told not to comment by either giving a good or bad report on his behavior or problem. She said, "We will take care of the inside, and when the inside is right, the outside will take care of itself." With the assurance that it was all right and he had been specially asked to attend, he agreed to come.

Each Sunday afternoon, I was surprised as each of our sons walked in the door. They were all faithful to our family meetings. At first, my reluctant son came in at the last possible moment. He sat near the front door, on the floor, and looked like he was ready to bolt out the door at the least provocation. He carried a small cooler filled with beer that he defiantly kept at his side. Slowly over the weeks, he began to come early and placed his beer in the refrigerator. Then months later he wouldn't drink while we were having our meeting.

Following Mother Mary's instructions, I made no comment with my voice or my face. One of the most difficult things to do is monitor your facial expressions. I knew I'd succeeded when one evening he called to inquire why I was mad at him. I asked him why he thought I was angry. He said, "You haven't been on my case about my drinking." Before our family meetings, I had done all the wrong things, using bribery, nagging, and guilt.

When I had realized I couldn't say anything about his drinking, I thought I would get more information on alcoholism from AA. I called Alcoholic Anonymous and said to the man who answered, "I have a son who is an alcoholic and I want to know how to get him to stop drinking." Without missing a beat, he said, "Attend Al-Anon." Well here was a big problem for me . . . I had to leave my home in order to attend. I prayed about this and asked for help in getting to a meeting. There were times I could dress, leave the house, and attend a meeting. Those times were blessed, because I found out that Al-Anon was a sharing with people who understood my situation. I learned a great deal about being co-dependent and how I had neglected my own life. But then, there were the other times I could get half-dressed and go no further. There were also the times I dressed, and then I'd sit in my car, not able to start it. I had times I could get dressed, drive to the site, and not be able to get out of the car. Believe me, during these times I was in constant prayer. I prayed for days to be able to attend, then I prayed my way through whatever happened.

Late one night, a year after we began to meet as a family, the phone rang; it was my daughter-in-law. My son wanted me to go to another area of town to drive him home. He was in a motel, too drunk to drive, and he was asking me to go after him. Having learned my lesson through Al-Anon, I said, "I don't do that any more" and hung up. But I couldn't go back to sleep, my eyes wouldn't stay shut. I woke Byron and told him what I was going to do. He said, "Honey, you can't walk out the front door in daylight, and you want to go that far, in the middle of night?" He encouraged me to go back to sleep and assured me that David could take care of himself. My eyes still wouldn't stay shut, and the feeling was of desperation . . . I just had to go get him. Later my daughter-in-law told me that David had said on the phone that night, that if I came to get him, then he would know that it was time for him to enter rehab.

At the motel, as I was struggling to get David into the car, he gave me his big pronouncement. He said, "Mom, I have something to tell you I never wanted you to know. I'm an alcoholic!" At the time I didn't appreciate the profoundness of his announcement and responded with, "No shit, David" as I continued to push, shove, and maneuver this drunk into the car. Although we all knew he was an alcoholic, it was the first time he had admitted his problem. The next day he entered a rehabilitation hospital for one month of treatment. On the way to the hospital, David said, "I know that you and Granny have been praying for me to stop drinking for a long time. It's taken me one whole year of daily prayer to have the courage to do something about my drinking." He has been sober ever since. He reminds me that he is an alcoholic and could drink again. He asked that I help him pray. This is how he prays, "If I should drink again, I pray that I will have the strength and courage to start back at step one, the next day." Now I, too, pray this prayer, not only for my own son, but for all people who are recovering from any addiction. Truly Mother Mary's words were truth. We took care of the inside, and through David's example we see that the outside will take care of itself.

With Mary's encouragement I've learned to listen to my inner guidance, which speaks to me through my heart. Often my inner guidance will say to me, "pray," when I feel there is nothing I can do to help, either a family member, friend, or someone who has written or called to ask for prayer. Mother Mary says that we should pray first and foremost. It's the best thing we can do to help anyone. I don't tell people I'm praying for them. I remember what

Jesus said while he was on earth about going into the closet and praying in secret, and allowing God to answer. I simply say the words, "I pray for David," or I give whoever's name I'm praying for at the time.

I've learned to pray without ceasing, allowing my heart to speak its concerns, and to allow one second for my mind to clear at the very least—more time is preferable. The beliefs I held in the past were erroneous and based on fear. Today I enjoy a relationship with "the Father within," as Jesus referred to God. I've come to rely on The Divine Parent who is loving, gentle, understanding, and above all, patient. Mary and the Brotherhood have taught us to change from the inside out. Jesus has taught me that God has a wonderful sense of humor and uses it to answer my questions and prayers in unexpected ways, and through the most unexpected means. I've learned not to take this life so seriously, but at the same time, to be very serious about my relationship with my Creator. But most of all, I've learned to pray in many different ways, to understand that, as Mother Mary says, "Prayer is talking to God and meditation is simply listening." I've learned that God doesn't need my prayers . . . I do. I've learned that the best gift I can give anyone is to pray with and for them.

Prayer is the lifeline of our existence on earth. It replenishes us in mystical ways; it quenches our thirst for truth and gives us a way to maintain hope. My prayer is that this collection of lessons and thoughts are as helpful to you as they have been to me and my family.

Annie Kirkwood

INTRODUCTION

A year after the book, *Mary's Message to the World,* was released, I was instructed by Mother Mary to go out and encourage people to live Her message. Often I give workshops along with lectures, and there is always time for questions. Many of the questions have been about prayer and meditation. I'll share some of the questions along with thoughts, ideas, and perceptions that I've gathered during the time I've been trying my best to "live the message."

Keep in mind that through these words, I am sharing what I've learned by doing this work. This in no way means that I think that I have the "right way" or that only my insights are correct or better than anyone else's. I don't have a great educational background, so I must rely on my own experiences and perceptions to share what I've learned.

No matter what the workshop is about, two questions seem to come up again and again . . . prayer and forgiveness. The first lessons I learned from the Brotherhood and Mary were that I needed to expand my definition, concept, and perceptions of God. I was told over and over, "God is much more than you can conceive or imagine." When I felt unloved, I was told, "God is so much more loving and forgiving than you believe." So I worked with this thought by repeating these words over and over, until at last I understood that I didn't have a good concept of just how loving God is. When it finally began to sink into my fear-ridden brain that God loved me more than I could ever know or could ever imagine, then my real healing began to unfold in miraculous ways. It then became easy to talk to a loving Parent. I think of God as not only our Creator but my Loving Parent, who is both maternal and paternal, filled with more love than we can possibly conceive, and more totally whole than we can imagine. He is All. God is everything that we know and everything that we don't know.

In order to impress upon my inner self how much God loves, I use affirmations. The first thing I learned about affirmations was that they were for my benefit and didn't in any way change God or God's mind. When I first began to use affirmations as a part of prayer, I thought that if God understands what I want, and how bad I want it, He will give it to me. This meant that I didn't want to change, but I did want to change God. God doesn't have to change. He is whole, total, and complete. We are constantly changing, with and without our awareness. It's part of the evolution of mankind. We, as part of mankind, are evolving into whatever comes next for mankind.

When I really began to feel that what I was affirming was true for me, then things changed for the good. I deeply and totally believe that God is my Source. He is the source of all that I need and/or want. God is my Health. As I've met health challenges, I realized that it wasn't God who was keeping me from being completely healthy, it was me. At first I thought God would wave a magic wand, and once He waved it over me, I would feel better than I've ever felt in my life. At first there was a lot of disappointment when I didn't achieve total health. And when a recurring chronic problem would rear its head, I thought I wasn't worthy. Then, through therapy, I understood that I didn't feel worthy or of value, period! Along with therapy, one of the methods I used was affirmations. I would repeat over and over, hundreds of times a day, "I am worthy; I am of value." At first this wasn't true of me, so I would affirm, "I am of value to Mark, or Byron, or David, or James." I knew that I was of value to Mark, my retarded son, who is completely dependent upon me. Mark only knows how to love. He doesn't evaluate or grade. I knew with my whole heart that I was of value to my husband Byron. He was the one who taught me what it is to be loved. He taught me that someone who loves you, wants the best for you. I also knew that my normal sons, David and James, valued me even if I didn't value myself. So I affirmed over and over, "I am of value to . . ." Slowly my self-worth was raised. Slowly I began to understand that God loves unconditionally. I didn't need to earn His love. He loved me just as I am, at any given time. Finally the day arrived where I could honestly say without reservation, "I am of value."

I feel it's important to fully "know" and "understand" how very much we are loved before we can become comfortable with prayer, at least that's been the case for me. Once I really "knew" deep in my heart that God loved me unconditionally, prayer and meditation were a lot easier. This precept then allowed me to understand that nothing is withheld from us when we are really and fully ready to receive.

One of the questions asked repeatedly is, "Why doesn't God answer my prayer?" I'm saying that God always answers. But how He chooses to answer may not be as we had first thought He would. When you pray, usually you have a good idea of what it is you're asking for. You probably have a definite idea of what it will look like, what it feels like, and how you think this will be. But sometimes God answers our prayers in different ways than we first imagined. For instance, some years ago I began to pray that my children would have happy marriages. I didn't know if their marriages were happy or not; they seemed content. I knew that I wanted them to be happy because I've been happy and at peace with Byron. In my thinking, I thought God would strengthen their marriages and would just fix any areas that needed fixing. I was not completely surprised when my son's marriage failed, who is a recovering alcoholic. After all, they had married when both were abusing alcohol and drugs. So when they sobered up, they were different people than they had been. But when my younger son's marriage broke up, it was a complete surprise and made me very sad. It dawned on me that maybe this was the answer to my prayer for their happiness.

I don't think that my prayer alone was the cause of their failed marriages, but I think that perhaps in order for them to have peaceful and happy marriages, they had to have something to work with. It takes two to make a marriage, and it requires two healthy individuals to have a happy and giving relationship. It also requires two individuals who love each other very much and who are willing to commit to working through problems. I also feel that relationships, and especially marriages, are so complex that often we don't have a full understanding of all that goes into making a good one work. But I do think that God is answering my prayer that my sons have a happy marriage, in His own way, and in His own time. I also pray this same prayer for my former daughters-in-law. I love them as daughters and want them to have good relationships and marriages, if that is their choice.

What I've learned is that God has a wonderful sense of humor. I feel that He answers my prayers in unexpected ways to keep me on my toes. If things were to go just as I thought they should, where would the challenges be, how would the excitement come? There have been times I've received an answer to a question or prayer through a song. I was thinking about love one day as it pertains to marriage and relationships, and how people go about looking for love. I'd been thinking about a country-and-western song whose lyrics say, "Looking for love in all the wrong places"; then I heard this song on the air. The song that immediately followed was Whitney Houston's song. "The greatest love I've found, I found inside of me" were the words that struck me as the answer. The greatest love is Divine Love and that love is found only within. Jesus said, "The kingdom of heaven is within." That is where the greatest love is found, within ourselves. We must first have love in order to be able to give it or share it with another human being.

There have been times my questions or prayers were answered through a newspaper article or something that was overheard in passing. There have been times that I realized that God answered my prayer, just as I asked, but not what I assumed He would give along with the request. Then there have been times God has answered my prayer just as I stated, along with how I envisioned it, with all that I assumed would be included.

Mother Mary has always instructed me to pray for myself first, then my loved ones, and then the world. I always took the words, "the world," to mean everyone else who came to mind, and for the planet in general. At first I thought praying for myself first was being egotistical and self-centered. But now I think it gets the things that are worrying or concerning us out of the way quickly and leaves us better able to focus on others.

Often I'm asked if Mary says there is a right or correct way to pray. She has said over and over, "Prayer is talking to God." What I've found is that I talk to God in many different ways. When I'm worried and very upset, I may beg or plead with God. When I am grateful, I seem to be filled with a sense of gratitude that is joyful. I go around saying, "Thank you, thank you," over and over. When I am afraid, I will fearfully ask God to help me. When I am confused, I say so. I've felt that God knows what is in my heart, and to try to deceive Him is ridiculous. So I tell Him the obvious and say all that is in my heart and mind. It helps me to speak out loud the worries and concerns, and feel that I am handing them over to my Higher Power/God.

In workshops and lectures I tell people, "Look for your answers to come in unexpected ways, through unexpected sources, and at unexpected times." Also, remember that we may not always recognize an answer at first; it's hindsight that allows me to see that truly an answer was given. Remember the old adage, "Be careful what you ask for, you may get it?" To me this means, think carefully about what you ask for or what you pray for. Be sure you have thought over exactly what it is you desire. You could get just what you asked for. I'm not sharing this to scare you, but to cause you to think about the times you felt your prayers were not answered as you wanted. Did you ask for what you wanted? Did you state your request in such a way there is no doubt what you are asking for? Or did you assume that God knew what you meant?

Understand that at times we get just what we asked for and that your prayer could be answered in unexpected ways. As an example, when my husband Byron was out of work and had been for a good while, I was going crazy having him underfoot. I was saying things like, "God, please get this man out of my house." When I told my friend, Anita, what I was feeling and saying, she reminded me that God could answer by literally getting Byron out of the house permanently, through an illness or even death. This was like a two-by-four hitting me on the head. I had a rude awakening to what I was letting myself in for, if I persisted to ask without voicing what I meant. I thought about what I wanted and then prayed, "God please find Byron a job, where he will go to work for eight hours a day and then come home afterwards." God answered my prayer. The only job Byron could find was working for minimum wage at the local Radio Shack. This after he had been earning a six-figure salary in the computer industry. Then I realized, I got just what I asked for. I had failed to request a good salary to go with the job.

In the past when I prayed for my loved ones, I began by trying to decide what it was they needed. This was very presumptuous of me, to think I knew what they should, or would, need. As I worked on my co-dependency issues, I found that it wasn't up to me to decide what they needed. In fact, I would never be able to know what was in their heart of hearts, so I could never have enough information to make these kinds of judgments. Besides, many things are choices, and I couldn't, and didn't want to, make their choices for them. Now I just simply say, "God, I pray for David, or Byron; help them," or whomever it is that I pray for, realizing that God knows their choices and their inner workings. He knows what we have need of and what we are choosing to have in our lives.

At first, I had the most difficult time trying to decide what it is I choose. I'd agonize over my choices, thinking that I would, or could, make a wrong choice. But both Mother Mary and the Brotherhood have assured me that I cannot make a wrong choice. Choice is just that . . . my choice. If I decide later that a choice I've made in the past is not working, then all I have to do is choose again. This way of thinking then led me to consider that I needed to let God know what my choices were. So after I have spent time going over my choices, I will have what I call a "formal conference" with God. I do this once or twice a year. I sit and talk out loud, because this helps me to hear my choices and to use more of my senses. I tell God what I want to have in my life and what I wish to have in my future. I describe the conditions I would like to have in my life and the situations I would like, but always I leave it to Him to fill my request with what is for my highest good. This goes along with the lessons I've learned about leaving everything to God. I say, "These are my choices, this or something better, Lord, is what I choose."

What I've found is that when I surrender my choices to God, and let Him work out the details, it is much better than I had dreamed of. Surrendering is one of the most difficult things I do. First, I agonize over my choices, and no matter how much I tell myself that I will not agonize, it seems that I do anyway. Then I pray over my choices, asking that if there is an alternative or better way to have the condition or circumstance that I choose, then to please let me know. I also pray that if something better is in the offering, that I can recognize it immediately. After a few days of praying in this way, I will sit down and write out my choices. Then I have my special conference with God when it feels like the right time. Afterwards, I trust. When I find myself doubting and trying to work out the problem for God, I remind myself that I am in the trusting phase now.

My job is to trust God, because He loves me unconditionally and can see how best to answer.

In my opinion, there are certain steps to take in making my formal request known. I must first choose and decide what it is that I want, remembering to include it all. Through past experiences I know that I will get what I ask for, but sometimes there are things that I've overlooked or assumed would be a part of the request, which were not. For instance, when I was a single mother, I prayed for a car that ran. I had an old Pinto that was constantly breaking down and costing me money to repair. I found the cutest, yellow Volkswagen Rabbit. I bought it, and it ran well. But one afternoon while I was at work, it began to rain. The orderly went out to close everyone's car windows. He returned and said, "Annie, where are your windows?" I said, "They are where they are supposed to be; they are not electric, and you have to roll them up." He replied, "No, honey, you don't have any glass in the windows. I see one is off the track, but the other one doesn't have any glass at all." I had bought a car that ran well. I assumed that if the car functioned well, that meant all its parts were in place and operated properly. So part of deciding, or choosing, is to be sure that I ask for what I want in such a way that nothing is left to chance. I want to leave no detail unstated, assuming that God knows what I mean.

Then, I pray that I can see this request from all angles and that I know what it is I'm asking for. I pray that if there is something better I'm overlooking, I'll see it now. There is also the request that I state clearly what it is that I want. I've had a problem of not being able to voice my needs. It seems to be tied to past incest issues in some way. It's almost like I thought I wasn't good enough, or smart enough, to be able to make choices or to have my needs met. It's still a problem for me to know what my choices are, but not as difficult as it used to be. This, too, is my prayer—to understand what my choices are. I will write them down and look at them, and pray over them for several days or several weeks.

Then, when it feels right, I have my special conference with God. I let Byron know that I am not to be disturbed until my session is over. He knows this is a special meeting with God. I talk to God as if I could see Him. I set a chair near me and talk to it, realizing that the chair is a symbol of the place within me where I'm connected to God. I tell God all that is in my heart, not only my requests, but my concerns and fears. I ask for help in overcoming my fears or to see how to handle them. When I end the session, I surrender it all to God. It's as though I were giving a report to my employer and, when I'm finished, my job is done. All I have to do then is to wait for my requests to be answered. The wait is fun, because then it's the anticipation and excitement of looking for the answers.

Next comes a difficult step for me, that of trusting. My friend, Anita, who teaches prosperity and abundance workshops, often reminds me that, "It's not any of your business how God works; it's God's business how He answers." So I've used this as an affirmation: "It's not my business how God will work this out; my business is to trust."

Learning to trust God took some doing, because I didn't trust anyone. Coming from a background of childhood sexual abuse, I learned early not to trust. I had to learn to trust myself and God. Many times, I knew that I was worrying, but I told God, "This is as close to trust as I can get right now. I am trusting . . . it may look like worry, but I am trusting now." What I think is most important in prayer is honesty. When we are honest with ourselves, and with God, then I feel that doors open within us and we are privileged to receive new awareness and new insights.

I'm often asked, "How do I surrender?" As I just shared, to arrive at that place where I can truly surrender is one of the difficult things about prayer for me. I asked Mother Mary, "How do I live this message," after she told me this was what she wanted me to do. Her reply is what I tell people about many things, including the difficult task of surrendering. Mary said, *"Do it as best you can."* When we do our best, and we know this is our absolute best, then God or Spirit takes over and helps us complete our task. My way may not be the way that works for you. I can only share some of the things I do. I pray for help in surrendering; I pray for a change of attitude; and I affirm over and over that I am in the process of surrendering. Since I believe I must be honest with myself at all times, if I were to say I am surrendering before I am, I would have funny feelings and think that's not completely true. But when I say I am in the process of surrendering, then I know that's my goal, and I am working towards it in my own way. So my answer is: pray, affirm, talk to yourself, and then talk to God in a very formal way. Then surrender your request, telling Him you are ready to surrender.

Mother Mary and the Brotherhood refer to automatic prayer. It seems that at times we pray without making a formal request. But one thing I've noticed is that it must be heartfelt. It takes the energy or emotion that is felt deep within my heart before I see results. An example of this happened recently. We moved from Dallas, Texas to Bunch, Oklahoma in August of 1995. Bunch is a very rural location, and we drive two miles along a dirt road to get to our home. Along this dirt road, which goes up a ridge of the Ozark Mountains, the scenery is very wooded. Since we moved here last August, I've been noticing some very large boulders, which are covered with moss, in the woods. Each time I notice them, I've had the heartfelt desire to have one or two in our yard. But I felt we could never move them, because of their large size and our lack of equipment, so I put it out of mind. Then I looked out my front window at a spot in the yard that has a raised flower bed. I've thought wistfully that one or two of these large boulders would be the perfect thing to sit on, to meditate outside. I've also had the idea of using the boulders as sculpture or unusual formations to make our garden and yard more interesting.

A few days ago, the man and son who does our yard asked Byron how I would feel about having an unusual rock in a flower bed they had cleaned out. Byron knew of my desire, because I'd commented on it numerous times. He too agreed that he had thought about having a boulder in our yard. It seems that our neighbor likes rocks and often finds rocks that "have character," according to him. He offered to bring the rock to us and set it in the flower bed. I told him of my desire to have two large boulders to sit on and where I wanted them placed. He said there was no problem and he would see to it. A day or two later, I realized that a prayer had been answered. This was not a request, but more of a wistful, yearning prayer not voiced. These kinds of answers to prayers are the most startling. How it works, I'm not sure. But I think it has to do with having a heartfelt desire, stating it to yourself, and then releasing it. I'm still working on understanding how this works for me.

One other comment about automatic prayer. I realized that worry was an automatic prayer. Since worry was something that was deep-seated, it was difficult for me to stop. I prayed to stop worrying. As I looked back at my family of origin, I realized that I came from a family that loved to worry. I remember my grandmother would start many a sentence with, "I was so worried . . ." My mother worries about everything. I learned to "what if" until I was filled with worry. In my lectures, I say that I came from a family that could have given medals for worry. It was such a part of our way of relating to each other. So working with the idea that worry was my automatic prayer, it came to me that perhaps since I couldn't seem to stop worrying, I could worry in a different way. Byron would ask me when I was deep in worry, and going over all the "what if's" as if it would all be terrible, "What if everything goes well?" With this thought in mind, I began to worry about what if everything went well and nothing unforeseen happened to stop whatever event I was worrying about. It certainly changes your perspective to worry this way.

On automatic prayer, I think it's important to understand that it is a part of our life and that we do pray even when we think we are not. It's important to trust that God brings only good, to remember that He loves each of us unconditionally and therefore whatever happens in my life is for my good—even when I've fallen and broken an ankle or a leg.

MEDITATION

In *Mary's Message to the World,* Mother Mary describes meditation as listening to God. There are many ways to meditate, and all of them are good; however, I suggest you do a couple of things first. Our family was taught to state our purpose for the meditation in the beginning of each meditation. There are taped, guided meditations, music for meditation, videos, and there is the concentration on a word or sound. My son David says that he can meditate as he runs. He runs several miles a week and finds that after awhile he is able to run and meditate at the same time. I'm sure the same thing is possible when you walk for a prolonged period of time. Some people worry that they fall asleep when they meditate. Think about this . . . when you give your spirit self direction, through stating your intention and purpose, then it knows what is expected and can comply. It's our conscious mind that falls asleep.

Meditation is a mindset, a period of time set aside to become still within. It's also the stilling of our mind, body, and whole self. Mother Mary says there are as many ways to reach God as there are people on Earth. He connects to us through that part of us that makes us different from any other human being.

As I've talked to people across the country, they tell me they find meditating difficult. I think that we have all been meditating in our own way all our lives. When we ponder or muse, we meditate. When we deliberate and when we reflect, we are meditating. Maybe we hadn't thought of these thought processes as meditation, but they are. Meditation isn't something new or mysterious; it's how we have always thought deeply on some topic. As I reflected on this, I found that when my conscious mind has given a topic or subject all my consideration, there is a period of time when all thought stops. It's those few seconds that God/Spirit uses to infuse us with the knowledge that we seek.

When people hear the word "meditation," and it's a new word or idea for them, they become confused. Perhaps remembering the 1960s and the "Let's get groovy" idea of meditation. Or they associate meditation with taking drugs and doing things that are considered illegal, immoral, and indecent. Others are reminded of the great yogis of India who sit upon beds of nails and go into a trance. Think back to when you first heard the word "meditation." What was the picture that came to mind? What was the feeling that you felt then? As you gathered new information concerning meditation, you changed your mind, but did *you* change?

People's preconceived ideas about meditation and what that is supposed to feel like, look like, and/or be, can be a deterrent. Once we have determined how a meditation is supposed to be, we are disappointed if it is different. Your meditations will be what they are. As you continue to meditate, your meditations may change. Please don't fall into the trap of comparing your meditations to anyone else's. How others meditate may not be the way you do. For instance, in the beginning of my meditating, I found it was best for me to meditate late at night, after everyone was asleep, when the city was quiet and it felt like things were muted. Later I could meditate in the morning, if I had a candle, music, incense, and I was sitting on one certain spot on my sofa. I wanted Byron to join me and get the deep feeling of peace that I received. He tried and it didn't work for him.

Later he tried to get me to meditate with him. He likes to darken the room, put on a tape of ocean sounds, get into his recliner and cover up. I argued with him that he was taking a nap, since he meditates after his noon meal. I said he was taking a siesta and not meditating. So I began to pray that Byron would be able to meditate with me— meaning that I wanted God to make Byron enjoy and receive just as I did. Some weeks afterwards, Mother Mary said, "Let Byron meditate the way he wants. His way will not be your way, and your way will not be his. Each will access God and Higher Knowledge in his own unique way." Then I had to stop teasing him about his siestas and acknowledge that he really was meditating his own way. The important thing to note about Byron's meditations are that he states his intention to meditate and connect to God-Mind before he begins. For a previous issue of our Newsletter, Byron wrote an article titled, "How to Meditate for the Spiritually Dense." This has been included as an Appendix for those who might find it useful.

Byron occasionally gets information and guidance in a clear way during his meditations. Most of the time he says he receives nothing. But we both know that the guidance can come later, and once again we look for it through unexpected sources, in unexpected ways, and at unexpected times.

Meditation is a learned skill, like riding a bicycle. The more you do it, the better you become. Also, try out new ways to meditate: concentrating on a word, self-guided dialog, using music in the background or nature sounds. You can try different times, until you find the most comforting time of the day or night. My family likes voice-guided meditations, when we come together as a group. It's similar to imagery. The task of guiding the group meditation seems to fall to me. After they have been led to go within by concentrating on their breath, I guide us to either an inner temple or a place in nature of their choice.

In the beginning this is exactly how I meditated. In my mind, I talked myself through my meditations, either to an inner garden or temple, where I could be silent and commune with God and all that is Good. What I now do most often is simply to get quiet and go within. Immediately I feel like I am on an escalator that takes me slightly up an incline and definitely within. I see colors, shapes, and splashes of lights. Sometimes I hear a voice, or receive a clear vision, but not often.

There are many reasons to meditate. The Brotherhood and Mother Mary have instructed us to have a purpose or intention for each meditation. We were taught to state our purpose or intention before beginning each meditation. Sometimes a meditation can be for the purpose of receiving an answer to a question or some other type of information. For instance, one day Byron received a call for a particular form that he had stored away fifteen years before. He recalled it, but couldn't remember where it was. Fifteen minutes into his meditation, he knew where it was. He found it in a box with papers from a business he had owned fifteen years before. He went into the garage, reached for the correct box, and pulled it out. He quickly found the paper the first place he looked. The people who had called were impressed. They had given him plenty of time to find it.

At times you can receive answers through your meditation. But remember . . . God has a sense of humor and could easily answer you much later and in unexpected ways. Most of my meditations are for the intention of communing with God. In these meditations I have no specific purpose other than to keep my connection to Him open and working. It's a most wonderful way to spend a few minutes or an hour or so.

Here are some of the questions that have been asked: I don't seem to be able to meditate. Nothing happens when I do. Answer: Once again let me remind you that Mother Mary says meditating is listening to God. One of the hardest concepts for me to accept was when *Mother Mary said, "God speaks to you in a silent voice."* I thought long and hard about this. To me this means that I will hear nothing. If it is silent, that means it's not heard. But it doesn't mean it's not real. A dog whistle makes a sound only a dog can hear. Perhaps this is what She meant. Our inner self hears, but our conscious, logical mind will not hear. After I understood how there was silent sound, or sound waves I couldn't hear, then I was comfortable with the premise of God speaking in a silent voice. This means we will not hear anything with our outer or inner ears. It is just silence and beautiful. God will address our purpose or intention for the meditation in a way that is most beneficial. I'm told it takes God seconds to infuse us with all the knowledge we need for a lifetime. So, if you can only quiet your mind for a second or two, it's okay. You've accomplished a lot.

Question: I try to meditate but I don't understand much regarding meditation and have yet to experience anything unusual. I have a lot of deep pain; is this preventing me from having success in my meditations?

Answer: I've explained that meditation is listening to God and that He speaks to us in a silent voice. I used to believe that I had to have unusual experiences during a meditation. Mother Mary told me that what I was looking for in unusual experiences was phenomena. She said we do experience phenomena at times, but to seek phenomena is to look for the sun rays instead of the sun. Phenomena is fun, exciting, and really makes us feel we are connected. When I first began to meditate, I looked for phenomena (didn't know what it was yet). I sought to have some unusual experience as proof that I had reached or achieved success. I tried very hard and worked at it. After a time, and with much practice, I began to have small, unusual experiences. At the same time, Byron wasn't experiencing anything. Since I've been able to hear Mother Mary and Jesus, it wasn't difficult for me to "hear" my inner guidance. I didn't consider the ability to hear unusual. I was looking for fireworks and/or blissful experiences. These types of experiences didn't happen. Now I consider my unusual experiences to be those times I really feel soul satisfaction and truly connected to love during a meditation.

Another thing that comes up with this question is the issue of worthiness. God loves us unconditionally, as Mother Mary assures us over and over. That means we don't have to be worthy or good enough to have a connection to Him. If we don't feel worthy, it usually means we learned to feel unworthy. We were either taught that we weren't good enough, or because we are so critical of ourselves, we don't feel worthy. These types of issues need attention and are often indicative of other problems. I have battled the issue of worthiness as a result of childhood sexual abuse. Through difficult inner work, I learned I wasn't bad or not good enough. Often parents who compare one child to another in the family will indicate that, from time to time, one isn't good enough. So look deep within to see where the issue of worthiness comes from, and if you need it, seek a good counselor. I have had a good counselor for years who has helped me tremendously to undo and resolve old hurts and pains. *Remember, we are all loved unconditionally.*

I received a call from a friend after we had been meditating together in a group. During the meditation I had the vision of Jesus laying hands on everyone to give a healing and Mother Mary greeting each person's spirit in love. I shared this with the group and thought they would like to know we had been visited. This doesn't always happen; in fact, it is rare that I see such visitations. My friend had driven home, she said, berating herself, thinking that she wasn't good enough to get to see such things. She said she quickly told herself this wasn't true, but yet there was still a little nagging feeling that maybe there was some small truth to the thought. This incident brought to mind the fact that some people hold on to their preconceived ideas of what should happen in a meditation. Preconceived ideas can act as a block to receiving our information.

Information doesn't always come to you in a meditation. For me, it usually comes in unexpected ways, and as

I've spoken to people, I find this is true for many people. When we hold on to preconceived ideas, we limit the way God can give us information, or we miss the information sent by not recognizing it. As I shared with my friend, we will not get a report card on earth. If you believe something indicates goodness, or indicates we have achieved a certain ranking in our spiritual progress, then you are in error. "This is not the real world," Mother Mary often says to me. "When you return to the real world, you will understand." This lifetime on earth is for practice. We are here to practice loving, forgiving, remaining at peace, trust, and faith. People who believe in good and evil have a need to grade and measure their progress.

Mother Mary says God loves. He loves unconditionally. Once, when I was asking how the Brotherhood ranked to the Angels, Mother Mary said to me, "Annie, there is only the Creator and His creation." This to me means there is no grading system for God. He sees us only as His creation and with love. If God loved us on condition, then there would be a real need for a grading system, a measuring tape, some way to see if we qualified for His love. Since God doesn't need to grade, measure, or qualify us in order to love us, we could say in the real world there is no measuring devices or grading system.

We are all created uniquely and individually. We are each beautiful in our own way. We are all qualified and good enough to be loved. Because we are all unique and individual, we each will have our own talents. We all have the same potential and demonstrate our spirituality in our own way. There is no way to compare ourselves to others. We each meditate in our own way and receive answers that are unique to us and individualized for our set of circumstances.

I'm often asked to say a few words about meditation and to give some suggestions. The number one suggestion is to throw out your preconceived ideas about meditation. As you begin your meditation, state your reason or intention for the meditation. Do your meditation at the same time every day. This could mean a specific time, like 6 a.m., or an unspecific time, as upon arising or before bed. When you get close to that time, your whole being begins to get ready. I feel that my body begins to slow down, and my mind begins to become quiet. Keep on practicing; the rewards are wonderful.

I hope these thoughts and insights help you. Please accept them in the spirit they are given. I'm simply saying that these are the things I've learned, and this is how I went about it. I don't wish to imply that what I've learned is the only way to go about it, or that it's the right way, or that I have a good handle on the subject. Perhaps through this sharing of my thoughts, something will act as a trigger, and you will receive an even greater understanding on the subjects of prayer and meditation.

Remember, Mother Mary says that God created each of us to be individual and unique in our own way. She says that it is through our individuality and our uniqueness that God connects to us. When I meditated on this for a good while, and pondered how God connects to us, I thought of snowflakes. Each snowflake is unique and individual, yet seen from afar they look alike. Humans, seen from afar, look alike. We all have two eyes, two ears, two arms and hands, two legs and feet, one mouth, one heart, and one brain. But in our personalities and in our own being, we are all different. Each of us is created with our own pattern and to be a wonder in our way. Each of us is beautiful because we are different and individual. This way of looking at our individuality makes me feel good. It once again says, we can't begin to imagine God's greatness or the immensity of His love. But loved we are and cared for in most abundant ways.

Annie Kirkwood

PART ONE

Awakening Your Soul

What Is Prayer?

In the beginning, when God set up the natural and physical laws of the Universe, He also set up your ability to seek His help. You call it prayer, but there is no magic in this word; it could be called petition or any other word.

The act of praying is not what sets up your answer. The repetition of your prayers at times helps you acquire the right mindset, but this is activated in your mind by the uniting of heart and mind.

When you have activated this mindset, then you will know what it feels like. It takes your desire, the agreement of your heart and mind, and faith that God will answer. The words or ideas of The Lord's Prayer are set up in such a way that they activate the opening of the switch, or the turning of the dial, to the answer of your prayer.

God is in the hearts and minds of those who do not fear Him and who welcome Him. Bring this Great Creative Spirit into your heart to fill your heart with all manner of good emotions—love, respect, honor, caring, kindness, compassion, peace, plenty, hope, and so much more. Bring God into your mind to help you discern the truth of all things. God is willing and able to show you the way to think correctly, but only if you invite His help.

Doorways to God

All religions are for people's benefit. The inner service of each religion gives you the feeling of Holiness. Each religion has some Truth, but the most crucial issue in all religions is the instructing in how to commune with God. The services are outer manifestations of what should be happening in your heart.

With your thoughts, attitudes, and longings, worship God. It is not by kneeling and praying in rote, without truly meaning the words you are repeating, that you worship.

The key is to give up everything to God.

This is what Jesus meant, not that you on earth should have more religions. Today there are already so many religions and churches, and still people are ignorant of where to seek God. It is not in a building, Mass, or religious service. It is not through your repeating of prayers in rote. *The only place to find God is in your heart, and in every mind is the door.*

Another mistaken idea is that there is only one door to God. There are as many doors as there are people, for each has in his own mind the door to God.

You should not look to any man, woman, or child to guide you to God, or to give the last word on how you are

4

to worship God. This is what is between you and God Himself—how you think, your attitudes, your beliefs, your way of facing life in general, and your internal worship of God.

Have you not thought that God is in your mind and your heart? He knows every thought, every hurt, every breath, every lingering feeling that is inside you. *There is nothing hidden from God.*

How to Pray

There is nothing you cannot ask God. He is Pure Energy, Love, and Wholeness. He wants you to talk to Him and to ask for His help.

Pray in your own way. Talk to God as you would a friend. You do not need to yell or holler; God is in your mind. There is no need for fancy words or for long pleas; God is in your heart and already knows what you have need of.

There is no need to tell anyone else about your prayers. These prayers are what Jesus made reference to when he said to go into the closet to pray. The closet is your mind. The closet is your thoughts. In a crowded room you can pray, in an instant you can pray, or for long periods of time you can pray, and no one need know.

All prayers are good. All prayers are heard. But remember that when you worry, you interfere in the arrival of your answers. So, place worry in God's hands.

Enter Your Inner Temple

Jesus taught that to make contact with God-Mind, you were to enter your closet and pray to God in private (Mt 6:6). God answers you openly, for all to see His power. The closet you are to enter is the closet of your mind. This simply means to go within.

Meditate and take your petitions to God in private, and allow God-Mind to decide what is best for you. You do not need to confess to man or to give your prayers over to anyone.

Do not give your inner instruction over to anyone else. Do not depend on another to receive your inner instructions. What you need to know will be revealed through you, but first you must practice the communication, and this practice is best achieved through meditation.

You must realize that the next century will be lived from the mind. Much of the new technology will have to do with the mind. Your scientists and educated will learn to use the great powers of the mind.

This is why we urge you to get a jump on this process by practicing it now. These great mental powers can be used now, but it takes practice. How do you practice or develop these?

They are a natural development of meditation. As you progress in learning to meditate, you will find yourself becoming more and more psychic. This is the best way to perfect these powers.

There is more to life than what is seen, heard, and felt. Meditate daily and give yourself time to consider your individual goals. It is important to build a temple in your mind. This temple will be a haven where you will find rest, comfort, and tenderness. The ability to enter your temple during times of pain and weariness is very beneficial to you. (On this day, during her morning meditation, Annie heard the words that are transcribed below):

When the storms of life are gathering around you and frighten and scare you, there is a haven in your mind, one that you've erected with your thoughts. This beautiful temple, which no one can see or enter, is for you alone. In the peace and love that warms you as you enter, you are ageless and weightless. You are all you desire to be.

In this inner temple of your mind is a connection to all energy, love, peace, health, wealth, and happiness. Herein lies the answer to all your prayers. In your beautiful temple is the door to God and everything.

Continue to modify your temple and to enter it on every opportunity to be relieved of worry and to be instructed. Talk to us in the Spirit world; we hear your thoughts when they are directed to us. But most important is to speak to God, who is in every cell in your body and already knows your thoughts and feelings.

It is all right to verbalize what you are thinking and feeling. God is very patient and will be happy to listen to you explain what He already knows. It is the turning to God that He looks for.

When you change your thought direction toward God, it is like setting the direction of your automatic pilot toward the supreme Good and your final destination. Perhaps you will delay to view and learn, but once you have set your sights on God as your destination and purpose in life, you will be Divinely guided into those situations that will give you the most learning in the least amount of time.

Set for your goal the meditations of the heart. Do not waver from this goal, for your very survival depends upon it.

In the coming decade, there will be many who will come saying their way is the right way to God. But if it does not lead you to an inner contact with God-Mind, then be very wary.

Be cautious in giving up anything of a spiritual nature to anyone. Jesus' method was of inner contact with God-Mind.

Open the Switch to Your Good

Begin with the concept of God that is in your mind. God is so much Greater, Grander, and more Magnificent than you can imagine. He is more Powerful, Tender, and Loving than you have imagination to use. Understand that you are like God, because you were made by Him in His Image and Likeness. The part of you that is like God is your Spiritual self. It is inside your soul that you look like God and where all of God's attributes are found.

Take with you the idea that God is gentle and can love you in ways which you know not. Allow these ideas to permeate your mind. Think on these words to aid you to find your own God-connection.

Make a commitment today—to work with God in everything, to open the door to your mind and heart to God, to be led by God-power alone, and to give God the opportunity to teach you in ways that will be miraculous to your eyes.

There is substance from which God can bring into your life all the good you seek for yourself and others. Now, as you desire this good, remember that what you desire for others is what you will be getting. So as you pray for yourself, always include others in your prayers, especially those who can harm you, such as criminals. Pray for relatives and co-workers. In this way, you open the switch to your good.

Prayer is a two-way street; as you pray for others, it will be done to you.

※ ∘ ※

Your Life-Line to God

As you seek God and set up the lines of communication, you are opening up the switches to have more and more spiritual good come into your life. Your mind will find ways to solve problems. New opportunities will come, doors will be opened and you will find an increase of All Good—All Good in the form of Pure Energy, which is God's Power.

As you ask God to help you understand and live this life, the highest and best way possible, you open doors that no one else could open for you. But one thing for sure, you will find that your motives, ideas, desires, and needs are changing. God can work with these changes. It's never too late to increase your spiritual learning.

And so, we urge you to keep the lines of your prayer life activated daily. This will insure your abilities to discern, to make good decisions, to see the truth in every situation and to "know."

In "knowing," you will simply not become swayed by any poll or anyone's opinion. You will not seek to find your answers among men, but in the very word of God, as it is given to your mind and heart. You will not look to any person for their viewpoint, ask for advice from another human or become indebted to anyone but God. And remember, God forgives your debts as you forgive your debtors.

This is our goal with you and with your lives. We wish only to instruct you in how to be happy, peaceful, prosperous, and healthy. Our aim is to connect you to God-Mind, which has all the answers and gives all good gifts.

$\not\approx \circ \not\Longleftrightarrow$

The Planting of Prayers

What we want you to do is to consider your requests as the planting time of the year. You enter your petitions to God through your prayers, and then you have faith that these petitions will be answered with what you have asked for, or better. In analogy, this is the springtime of your year, and it is the petitioning time for your needs, wants, and desires.

In the growing season of your earth, there comes the time to wait for the seeds to break out of the ground and to grow strong. This time requires you to do something. You must water, hoe the ground, and watch for insects and other animals who will take the young shoots, but mostly you are waiting and waiting for the fruits and vegetables to ripen.

Then the time of harvest comes, and there is much activity and more work than you can imagine. Soon all the work has been done, and the crops have been harvested and stored for the coming year. Then comes the time of reflection and planning.

Well, loved ones, the same events can be viewed in the prayer process. There is the time of planting, which are your requests. There is the time of waiting and of keeping the insects and animals from the crop; this is the time to use faith and watch your thoughts for any worry. Then it is the time of harvest, when your prayers are visible and usable to you. Later comes a time of reflection and planning. We will take each step slowly and give you pointers on how to be more effective in praying.

We will begin with the last. Remember Jesus' words to the effect that: the last shall be first and the first shall be last. This is a time of using the last part first, the planning and reflecting time. In this period of time, you are deciding what it is you need in order to live your life in comfort and peace. In what set of circumstances do you wish to live? Be honest and not extravagant. This is a serious time of reflection.

With God all things are possible, but in your mind you must ask for what is visible to you. When you ask God for a set of circumstances, can you actually see yourself living in these conditions, managing the lifestyle you would like?

Know that each set of circumstances requires its own payment. In order to have a business of your own, you must be willing to work hard to get it going and sustain it. You must also be willing to put aside your need for entertainment and enjoyment.

It is all work, for a long while. This is how you are to look at your chosen lifestyle.

Reflecting is simply a way to think. It means you are considering all the odds and all the evens to see the complete picture. Take this time, now, to plan each phase of your life. What do you truly want with all your heart? What are you willing to work for?

Start with your body and its appearance, then go to your career or job, your home and all your possessions, your loved ones. Make lists of what you desire, and think on these desires for a few days. Then make another list of what you are willing to have, with all its required payments in time, effort, sacrifice, and energy. Now you are ready to plant.

Next comes the planting time, or the time to seed your prayers with requests. Now that you have reflected and taken time to contemplate your earnest desires, you are ready to petition God and All His Abundance. Keep a list of your prayers in a notebook or tablet of some kind. Set the date of the petition on it, pray, and tell God simply, honestly, and sincerely of these requests. Get quiet inside yourself and feel the presence of God as He listens to your petitions.

Now comes the hard part, the waiting and keeping your hopes high. Now is the time to use statements of faith and to read inspirational books, and the Bible, about faith.

Reaping the Harvest

Now comes the fun part, the time of harvest and of reaping all your rewards of life. It is easy to be grateful when you are seeing the answers to your prayers, but be grateful always for these answers. It will be easy to tell God how grateful and how much you love Him at this time. Do so, and sing songs of Thanksgiving as they well up in your soul. This prayer of thankfulness should be one that is said daily.

Now you are back at the beginning of the process, the time of planning and reflection, the time to put into action your prayers once again. Of course, know that this is an ongoing process. Now is the time to change your mind, to change your request, or to perfect to your individual taste each petition.

Try this type of praying and see the benefits and rewards. It will not take much of your time, but it will take your being consistent in keeping hope and faith alive in your heart and mind. Of course this process is an ongoing occurrence.

Do keep a record of all your prayers. Change these prayers and requests as you wish. When you have your desires firm in your mind and you have maintained the faith and hope, then look for the answers to come.

The Powers of Prayer

Begin each day with a prayer, even if it is as short as "God help me this day." End each day with a prayer of gratitude. Remove the hard emotions that block your ability to reflect the attributes of God. We are not advocating that you ignore your outer life, but simply that you balance it with prayer and meditation. Ask God's help to eliminate the hard emotions and thoughts from the inner self.

Forgive all people and forgive the world. Forgive yourself; this is also important to your growth.

Return to a time of prayer for yourself, your goals, and your life. Then pray for the world, all people in the world, for all of God's creations. Pray to strengthen your connection to God.

Talk to God as you would a friend. There is no better friend. Be willing to change your inner self in order to be the person you desire to be on earth.

All is good, the inner life and the outer. All is to be balanced with prayer and through your communication with God.

Some of you feel that when we say pray, you think (in your own words) that this is "a cop out." This is not so!

18

Prayer is a powerful act. You invoke many old and ancient powers of good when you pray.

Prayer is automatic, in that it always gives good results. Perhaps you do not see the results as good at first, but have faith that good is what will be the outcome. Prayer will not give any other answer, it cannot. Prayer will help you grow; it will prevent you from making grave mistakes in judgment.

Good judgment is one of the powers of prayer. Judgment is good when you use judgment as God does, *to discern and decide.* Pray for the pure judgment of Truth to enter your life and give its good results.

Release your prayers to the Highest Power, which is God Energy. Allow it to work and bring the good that you expect. When you take your prayers back into your conscious mind and mull them over, you interfere with the Power of God, the power that could be handling your request. Resolve to pray with more feeling and to release your requests to God-Energy, which brings only good results.

Take your goals and pray on these daily. Release your goals to God-Energy to become a part of your inner life, which in turn becomes a part of your outer life.

When to Pray—and Why

Understand that the need for prayer is urgent. Ask God to help you with the praying. Tell Him everything that is in your heart. Learn to put aside the angers, fears, and hostilities that only add to the violence in the atmosphere.

I ask that each person pray one hour per day. Know that this hour can be broken into parts.

You may pray fifteen minutes in the morning or perhaps thirty minutes. You can then pray the rest of the time at night. Or you may pray for ten minutes in the morning, twenty minutes upon entering your home, and the rest before bed. See, this is how to set aside time for prayer.

Understand also that you can pray at work; when people think you are lost in your thoughts, you will be lost in God's world. Perhaps you can commit to praying only fifteen minutes per day. This is fine, but increase your prayer time as you learn to pray.

Pray for all people, for those you know and for those who are merely a part of this life on earth. Pray for your enemies. Ask God to help you forgive them. Ask God to bring into your heart thoughts of love for all people. Pray for those who have spoken badly about you, those who perhaps have been nasty or mean. Consider that they do not know their true worth as children of a loving God.

Perhaps it will be well worth your learning the prayer of Saint Francis of Assisi, he who asked God to make him an instrument of His will—to help him plant love where there was hatred, to bring peace where there was strife, to bring joy where there was sadness—see, this is how to pray.

There are many ways to pray. Take note of prayers that have endured the passing of time. If you cannot think of any other way to pray, repeat over and over The Lord's Prayer. In this way you will be opening up your mind to project good into the world.

Your thoughts are powerful, as are your words. Be careful how you use your thoughts and words. Make use of these powerful elements, which you alone control. Pray by speaking the words love, peace, and hope to all people and to all nations.

Unselfish Praying

Praying is speaking to God either formally, as in The Lord's Prayer, or informally. Either way, you are indeed praying. *It is a matter of heart and not of words. It is a matter of intentions and not simply phrases.* God can and does look into your hearts at the time of prayer and sees your true intentions.

To pray selfishly, you would want your needs, desires, and hopes met without anything being required of you, simply because you asked for it. You would never think of anyone else. Their desires or needs become unimportant. It is you, first and foremost.

Now, in order to pray unselfishly, you need to understand that everyone on earth has the same kind of needs and desires. What you think is important, everyone considers important for themselves. In praying unselfishly, allow God to give what you truly need and desire.

At times you do not know what you need or even what you truly desire.

Everything has a price! In order to pray unselfishly, you must be willing to pay the price. The price is not always in terms of money, but in terms of conduct or consequences.

This is praying unselfishly—when you allow God-Mind to make the final decision.

In this case, a selfish prayer would be, "I do not want to hurt for any reason, and please just take the hurt away, even if I do not learn anything." In order to pray unselfishly, she would say, "Give me the courage to withstand the pain, in order that I may forgive." God will answer the unselfish prayer first.

Understand God will wait for you to ask for His help. He will be waiting for you to call on Him. Remember always simply to talk to God in your own language, in your own words. This is true prayer. Worship and become One with God.

Bring God into Your Life

Communication with the Father is an ongoing process. It is like living life. To live life, you do not do it one day only and then put life on automatic pilot. You live daily in life, doing, thinking, and performing. This is true of your communication with the Father. There is no plan of salvation that would allow you to perform certain steps and then be saved for all time. *To be in true and open communication with your Creator is a moment-by-moment process. It requires you to question and seek to be near Him.*

Many people take it upon themselves to live life without the Father. Bring God into every part of your life and allow His Divine Will to be done.

Give Him your problems, but give them up completely. Give them to God the Father with the thought that you are happy and content with His Will. *Understand that God's Will is always Good. God cannot give anything but Good.*

※ ∘ ⁂

How Unconscious Thoughts Reproduce

All the words and thoughts that are in your mind are prayers. That is why it is important to watch these trains of thought and what you decree with words. How is this? Let me explain.

In your mind is the connection to God the Father. Through your heart is the other part to this connection. That's why I request that people do a good job of cleansing their minds and hearts of all depleting emotions.

A depletion of energy takes place when there is an abundance of fear, anger, envy, avarice, resentments, hatred, and all these types of emotions. Most are doing such a good job of cleansing, yet many have not realized that every thought and feeling is a prayer. What you think about and mull over in your mind becomes a meditation. What you feel when you are not conscious of feelings is a prayer.

Take a look at what is in your heart as feelings. Do you become easily upset? Do anger and fear well up within your heart when you're uncertain? What are your reactions to life situations? Is there some circumstance or person causing anguish? Do you concentrate on what is wrong? At times, do you feel separated from others and God?

In your mind, do you speak in a berating way? Do you become your worst nightmare of a parent? Are you concentrating on what is wrong in your life?

Do you read about violence and fighting? Do you go see movies and dramas about violence and warring? Does the thought that reproduces in your mind cause you to become upset? These kinds of thoughts are your meditations. Thoughts reproduce, and the unconscious thought reproduces faster because there is no rein to hold it back.

How to Pray for the Removal of Unconscious Problems

"Oh, Lord, I have this problem, _____." And it is repeated and repeated in detail in the mind. All concentration is on the problem and how terrible it is and how much worse it could get.

"Oh, what if . . . ?" These are the words that should set bells to ringing and alarms going off in your mind. No amount of "what ifs" will cure the problem. Seeing the worst of any situation will not alleviate it.

Pray and tell God in one short sentence what the problem is. Confess your inability to solve it. Ask for guidance and for help. Quiet your mind until you can gain a sense of releasing the problem to God.

Thank God for the answer to the problem, and continue to release the problem. When you are prone to worry, instead, remind yourself that this is in God's Hands and is being solved in spiritual ways. Soon you will see the results.

God's result in solving a problem always comes in the right way at the right time, and for the good of all concerned. Continue to thank God and ask Him to help you to increase your faith, for it is by faith that your prayers are answered.

Remember that Faith is the hope of the unseen answer to your prayer.

God Hears Everything

Prayer is not only the request made in a thoughtful way, but the thoughts that you think throughout the day.

In the past we have taught about automatic prayer and conscious prayer. The thoughts that run through your mind are automatic prayers. The reactions that spring up within your heart as feelings are also automatic prayers. Words are decrees. That is why it is very important to watch your thoughts, feelings, and words.

God hears everything. He has set up for much of what you think about to be brought to you without effort, automatically.

This is what I call automatic prayer. God is both Principle and Personal. As Principle, He sets many things in order, to run on their own. This world is a good example. No one needs to be concerned with day and night. Automatically one follows after the other. No one is in charge of tides or currents of the oceans. They follow their course.

Change the Worry Habit

Prayer is set up to run on what is kept in your mind and heart the longest. With this in mind, do you realize that worry then becomes a prayer? Worry is a bad habit, one that can be changed.

Now I will review the methods to change worry and the thoughts that are allowed to roam throughout your mind freely.

When you become aware of unwanted thoughts, simply say, "NO! NO! I no longer wish to have this condition or circumstance in my life. I thoughtfully choose to have these types of thoughts leave my mind immediately. This is what I will think of: _____." And then think what you wish to have in your life.

For instance, suppose you are worried about a loved one. Perhaps this person is ill in body. When you think of him, say in your mind, "He/she is healing beautifully now. I will not judge by the appearance of illness, but by righteous judgments of health, calmness, and love."

Or, if there is a coming event in your life of travel, if the thought enters of accident, say again, "NO! NO!" or "Cancel! Cancel!" Then say, "I no longer think in this manner, but see myself traveling in comfort and safety. God protects me at all times and is with me at all times." There are so many good examples. If the thought of lack of money comes to mind, remind yourself that "God is my Source. HE will care for me as HE does the birds of the air. Nothing I need will be kept from me." Later, if you continue to entertain thoughts of lack, these thoughts are what become true in your life.

Face Yourself in Truth

*G*od *sees into your heart, and there the truth of you is seen.*
Perhaps you have hidden the truth from yourself.
Perhaps you truly do not see anything that needs correct-
ing.

Pray that you may see the truth about yourself, because
only in truth can you see what needs correcting. Only by facing
yourself in truth can you grow.

It takes a big person to admit his mistakes. It takes one
who is mature and able to take self-scrutiny. This is a
requirement in order to mature and grow in spirit. Every
person on earth has an area that is in need of correction and
possibly elimination.

This is our lesson to you: *take time in your meditations to*
scrutinize your inner self, the self you show only to God.
This is the way to make amends, before any drastic event
brings you face to face with yourself.

Allow this to be your prayer for the next fortnight, to
take a good look at your own weaknesses, your own
behaviors, your own habits and your own thoughts, because all events proceed from your thoughts.

To correct a behavior may require help from people who are trained to help you. To overcome a bad habit perhaps takes the aid of others of like mind.

All corrections begin with prayer, with the desire to change. All bad habits are eliminated because of the individual's desire to put this away forever.

This theme of going within to look at yourself is one that is recurring in your Bible. Jesus gave many lessons on looking within.

To look within is to look to God and to look at yourself in reality.

Let each one correct his own mistakes and give others only your prayers.

Pray that you may see the truth about yourself, because only in truth can you see what needs correcting. Only by facing yourself in truth can you grow.

Prayer is the easiest way to change.

Give your attention to God and allow Him to guide you gently in the changes to make.

"Father-God, help me see myself as I truly am. Help me correct those areas in my life that are correctable, and help me accept those areas in my life that cannot be corrected."

"God grant me the courage to change the things I can, the serenity to accept those things that cannot be changed, and give me the wisdom to know the difference."

What to Do
When Nothing Changes

Be honest with yourself. In most cases, it's an old feeling of long standing which must be forgiven. One must forgive again, again, and again. Often the same person must be forgiven.

Forgive yourself daily for falling into old patterns of behavior, thinking, or feeling. Be gentle with yourself, and at all times love yourself into wellness. Wellness of mind and heart is how love will heal.

People say, "I pray and pray and meditate, and nothing changes." My children, if one doesn't watch over one's reactions and wandering thoughts, nothing will change. Wandering thoughts and unconscious words will automatically cancel your conscious prayers. Both must be brought into the Great Mind of God.

So, pray to change your wandering thoughts. Simply say, *"Father, help me discipline my every thought and clean my heart of all depleting emotions."*

Let this be your daily prayer. Let this be your constant reminder that every thought is a prayer and that every feeling brings into your life a repeat of itself.

※ ○ ※

You Can Choose to Change

Be cheerful and think of joy, love, and contentment. This is what you came to learn and practice. This will do much to improve not only your life, but the lives of those whom you love.

By accepting yourself with all your frailties and errors, you are accepting this process as your mission in life. When you become aware of unwanted thoughts, think, *"I am now cheerful, loving, and kind."*

When you become aware of unsettling feelings, say, *"From this day forth, I choose to feel loving, kind, appreciative, and joyful."* This will become a prayer as well as your feeling. You are the only one who can change your mind or your heart. You do this by choosing to change.

It's a gift of God to choose what to think and how to feel. Use this gift well: choose to love, forgive, and accept. Love, forgive, and accept yourself—God does.

Remember that God loves you, just as you are now, wherever you are on the road to perfection. He loves you however you think or feel.

He loves you because that's all God does—He LOVES at all times.

God's Definition of a Good Life

"I ask God the Father to help me with my life goals, those I have set up for this week, this year, this lifetime. I rely and trust God to help with all my goals."

"This is new and I do not know how to think of this. Help me learn the lessons I came into this lifetime to learn. Help me with my goals for this year, this week, and today."

So however you define a good life, if it agrees with God's definition of a good life, it is yours. Pray to bring God's definitions into your life. These definitions bring conditions which are good. God's definitions are love, illumination, light, courage, valor, trust, order, strength, happiness, joy, life, energy, power, wisdom, and much, much more. These are the very "things" you are striving for. These are the conditions you desire to have in your life. Now we teach you how to have them, how to attain your goals.

But we cannot do it for you. Neither will God, unless you ask Him to enter your life and aid you. God will help, but He will not do it for you.

Daily meditate and pray for God to help you grow in spirit and on earth. Ask for help to perform the task you have set. If you need to seek another job, do not go alone.

Go armed with God, Jesus, and us. We are all here to help you live daily. Remember that most problems can be overcome with a change of attitude.

Pray for knowledge of your life work and of issues that need to be resolved. Seek to help through prayer, because this is the best way.

Pray for what you desire, but release what you pray for to Spirit to work on and bring into your life the best for you. It is not important what you have, but how you learn the lessons associated with the events of your life.

Some have had experiences that have not been pleasant. There have been pain and disappointments. Understand, these come into your life for a reason. Seek to find the reason through prayer and meditation.

In your prayers, ask the Father within to give you understanding. As God releases His great Understanding, there is a release of energy which will benefit you in many ways, internally, spiritually, and physically.

How to Affirm the Truth

God relates to you in a personal manner by loving you, just as you are now and as you will be. You are given freedom of choice, and, in order to retain your freedom, God relates to you as Principle. That means He set up the Universal laws to work whether you believe in them or not.

These laws are automatically set into action with a thought or act. Before you entered into this life you committed to lifetime goals. You also made a "wish list" of all the things you would like to accomplish. You chose circumstances, places, culture, and named some vocational desires and educational desires.

Now, the educational desires were of life issues and not schooling. God the Father, as Principle, answers your prayers in life. What you concentrate on is what you receive. He is impersonal and unemotional about this, as principle. This way all people are given the desires of their hearts.

This requires you to concentrate on what you want and to make a decision. The decision is one that is made with your mind, heart, and soul.

Concentration, then, is the key to opening up to what you desire. It must be a *firm commitment* to what you desire, and it must not be harmful to anyone else in order for the good to come from God.

All the Good you desire is already prepared for you by the Father. His energy and creativity are constant and never ending. *There is no limit to God or His Supply.* When you receive from the Father, you are not in any way depleting His storehouse of good, nor will you be taking away someone's success, money, or health.

There is plenty for every person who has ever lived and who will ever live. Put out of your mind the thought that there is a limit to God or to His Good.

The ones to convince are yourself and the inner workings of your mind and heart. *These affirmations are not for God's benefit, but for yours.* God knows His potential. It is mankind who is ignorant of his potential. Therefore, it is your mistakes in reasoning that inhibit you.

I will show you how to release all old negative ways of looking at your life. *Your job is to convince your mind and heart that God is wanting to give and is willing to supply you with all kinds of Good.*

You can have what you desire, as long as this desire is in keeping with your own lifetime goals, and what you ask for will not interfere with your goals in this life, nor will it cause harm to you or anyone else. So, the following affirmations are for you. Use them to agree in your mind, heart, and soul with what you desire.

Always end each prayer time of affirmation with the statement of allowing God's Will to be done unto you.

When you can allow God the Father to perform His perfect Will in your life, all circumstances and all people will be put in your path without any worry or concern onyourpart. It will just simply happen before you know it.

First, I will list the areas of life that we will address. You will be solving old problems and bringing into your life health, wealth, and happiness.

You can bring into your life success, creativity, money, honor, and release from anything that would deter your growth.

Begin with statements of Truth about God the Father and you, such as:

- I believe in God, Creator of the Universe. I believe in Jesus, His son, and I believe that through the power of the Holy Ghost I communicate with the Father. I believe in Eternal Life, forgiveness of sins, and communion with all worlds.

- I release all fear, envy, resentment, and negativity from my mind, heart, and soul. I seek only Divine Love.

- My heart and mind are in agreement with God's perfect Will in my life.

- I request the Angel of Divine Love to enter my heart and heal me of all that deters my success in this life and my spiritual growth.

- Divine Love heals my body, mind, and heart. I go in peace, knowing that all is well.

- Divine Love protects me in all circumstances of life. I am Divinely Protected, Divinely Guided, and Divinely Healed.

- Through the Power of God the Father, I am capable of success in life by my definition.

- My Heavenly Father is supplying me with all the money I need to meet all obligations, the money to shelter, dress, and feed my family. I no longer fear receiving bills or fear any need for clothing or food.

- I am Divinely Guided into situations that will enrich my life with money, love, and peace.

- I stand in a circle of Divine Light to be healed of all ailments now.

- God is working His perfect Will in my life. I am at peace.

- God's Will is only Good, so I call on God's Will to be my will.

- I call on God the Father to place me in the right place at the right time, in order to be financially successful. God wants me to be a success by my definition. I release anything that hampers me from obtaining this success.

- I allow God's Will to spur me into action. I have all I need within me, to be all I want to be. I am grateful.

- Through the Power of God, I can be healed. It is God's desire that I live this life in perfect health. Therefore, I release all fear concerning my body, mind, or feelings.

- The Truth of God is opening my mind to all possibilities. I am healed in mind, body, and soul. I do not need to do anything in order to deserve this health; it is mine by the Grace of God.

- I can be loving, kind, and warm because I am filled to overflowing with God's Love. I am patient, kind, friendly, concerned with my world and myself. I will be kind, loving, and concerned with others, as is the Father.

- I seek to be in close communion with God in order to be all I want to be.

- I am always in God's Love, but I do not always know this. I will tell myself I am always in God's Love.

- I give the problems of this day to God to adjust and bring into order.

- I release all concerns to the Power of God, to set in Divine order. I walk this day in God's Light and am always in perfect tune with Him.

- I am a radiating center of God's Love, mighty to receive my good and share my good with others.

- All the good I desire is wanting to be in my life. I release anything that detains my receiving this good. I accept my good, and I ask that others realize that their good is waiting for them to claim it.

- I go forth this day in peace, love, and happiness. I am happy with my life, home, and family. All differences are ironed out in the Name and through the Power of God.

- This is the day the Lord has made. I will honor this day with a cheerful attitude, a happy heart, and a grateful mind.

- I am truly thankful for my life, work, and health. God adjusts every situation in my life with His love.

- There are angels who watch over my coming and going. I am always in the company of God's Angels. They are with me to help instantly with any need.

- I love the Lord my God with all my heart, all my mind, and with all my soul and strength, and I love my neighbor as myself.

- I send the Angel of the Lord before me to prepare my way. Every person I meet today is my friend. All my daily transactions are conducted in peace, and I am Divinely protected.

- I call upon the Angel of Love to heal this situation. My home, loved ones, and my life are healed now.

All these affirmations can be used for others simply by replacing the "I" with a "You are." This is the way to affirm for others healing, love, peace, wealth, health, and happiness.

Today, take these affirmations and your individual prayer list. Before beginning, make adjustments in the prayer list by adding names, and beside the name add one word to indicate what you are praying for, such as "Annie-health" or "Byron—protection in travel." Begin by declaring for yourself and then declare for those people on your list. Do this every day and see results.

Who and
What to Appreciate

Appreciate your partner in life. Understand that you can improve your marriage and life together, as you appreciate your mate and his or her work. As you see the good in your mate's eyes, you will see the love grow.

Appreciate your children. Appreciate the lessons these young ones are bringing to you as parents. You are learning patience, understanding, comprehension, and you have the opportunity to see the world through their eyes.

Appreciate the lessons, homework, teachers, fellow students, and all school activities. Appreciate your homes and possessions. Appreciate your parents. They may have their faults, but they also have their strengths. Like you, they are on this earth to learn life's lessons.

To the adult, married children, also appreciate your home and notice not what is lacking, but what you have attained. Appreciate your lives together and your work. Continue to pray for your loved ones.

Forgive your parents for being human, and understand that they did the best they could at the time. You too may soon become parents, and it is always good to treat others as you would like to be treated. How you treat your parents is how your children will treat you.

For those of you who are not married, appreciate your parents and see the love that is in their eyes.

Praying for Others

Each person is to pray, the one for the other, and never criticize or point out someone else's defects.

But in all honesty, one on one, you can tell the other what concerns you have about them. You can say, "I see in you this depleting emotion because I recognize it in me."

Love and pray together. As each of you corrects himself, you are helping all the people whose names are listed on your prayer list. Add to the list each week the name of the person who this week caused you to feel a depleting emotion. Add names as you meet people and as you get to know others. Soon your basket of prayers will be a large one.

All people whose names are listed on your individual prayer list will benefit by each step you take to heal your soul.

How to Pray for Home and Family

I ask God for the money to provide a good life for myself and my family. I pray for the money to buy my family the "things" it needs in order to live without a struggle. I ask for new opportunities to earn more money and to fulfill my creative and internal desires to succeed. This is a good prayer.

The best you can give anyone is your love, concern, and your thoughts of goodwill. The best, which are your thoughts of love, hope, and peace, and your prayers and meditations for each other. Pray for your loved ones—this is the best gift.

See, little children, prayer is more than simply requesting. Tell God-the-Father what concerns you about your loved ones. Is it that they are unhappy or ill in spirit? Tell God-the-Father all that is concerning you.

Use both kinds of prayers, the formal, such as The Lord's Prayer, and simply speaking to Him as a father. What concerns you about world affairs? Pray for this too. What concerns you socially? Pray for this also.

The best you can do for a loved one is pray. Remember that prayer is not your will being done for another, but your prayer is for good to come to this person.

Your Truth is individualized and will not be for anyone else. What you sense and what comes to you in your mind is your truth and guidance. It probably will not be right for anyone else.

So how do you help your loved ones?

—through prayer for their spiritual good.

—for the opportunity to give them joy and comfort.

—by praying to know the correct time and method to approach them with your truth.

—through using the correct words to tell them what you are feeling.

Prayer for Peace

"God, allow peace to reign in the hearts and minds of men, and allow this peace to first begin in my heart and mind. . . .

"This day I send my thoughts of PEACE to every man, woman, and child alive on this planet. I ask God to allow men to see His Peace in every nation and ask God to allow the leaders of nations to recognize His peace.

"I send thoughts of Love and Peace to my parents, brothers, sisters, spouse, home, workplace, to every person with whom I come into contact this day. I begin to think in terms of Peace. I seek Peace in my home and in my relationships.

"I send Peace out into the world and the entire Universe."

Continue to pray for the uplifting of the race consciousness. Pray for the world and the whole planetary population. *Ask for all world problems to be solved in a peaceful manner.*

Pray for a dying away of angers and an end to hostilities in the heart and mind of mankind. The war is over, but the anger, hatred, envy, and desires for power are still in the hearts and minds of many of the people in this part of the world. It is a powder keg of emotions which can be riled into aggressions again if not released.

Peace is lasting only when it has entered every heart and mind of the world's population. There is still danger in this part of the world and there is still a need for much prayer, not only for this immediate area, but for the surrounding nations. In the land of Yugoslavia, there is unrest and aggression in the minds and hearts of men and in many other areas of the world.

Meet in small or large groups to pray for peace, hope, and for love to come into every heart and mind, beginning with your own. Your prayers will meet the prayers coming from other places of the world and will act as a balancing of power in the race consciousness.

Remember that what you pray for is the uplifting of the spirit of peace, hope, and love in this world.

Pray that each individual on earth remember his Divine plan and be prepared to meet back here in spirit with a new attitude towards life. Pray for a new uplifting of race consciousness for the next era.

Prayer and meditation are your connection to God-Mind, and it will be through this connection that your life will be enhanced on earth and in reality.

Prayers for Every Circumstance

Physically: "I call on God for help to resist that which is detrimental to my health."

Mentally: "I depend on God to help me clear out of my mind all that inhibits my communion with God the Father.

"I pray to Father God to cleanse all that keeps me from reaching Him with a good, strong connection."

Ask Him to wipe out all memories that rear up from the past to cause you problems in the present. "Be with me as I make every decision."

Emotionally: "I place all my emotions in God the Father. I place all memories of hurt feelings, broken relationships, misplaced loyalty, of childhood hurts, in the Love of God, the Father.

"I ask God to help me increase my expectation of Your Good and Your abundance. I ask God to raise my viewpoint of how life can be lived."

"I ask God-Mind to help me elevate my standard of living today. God is in charge of my life; God is helping me meet these payments on time and with ease. I no longer feel hopeless or discouraged. My life is in God and in His Power to act instantly.

"God is in charge of me and all that affects me. My life, my body, my money are directed by God Himself."

Speak to the very circumstances, to the requests for payment, to the aches or pains. Tell them, *"You are not true. You are only an appearance of truth and not truth itself. My truth is God and His Power.*

"Father, I desire to have greater faith in order to receive all that has been prepared for me."

Next, pray to the Father who is within to help you in all ways, and then list the ways. Say, *"I need help in believing today, Father,"* if this is the case. Or, *"I need help in doing,"* or whatever your need is for that day. Ask for it. He is always willing to help, but because of freedom of choice, He waits for you to ask for help with sincerity and with earnestness.

"Father Creator, I am ready for all the Good you have prepared for me. I am ready with a grateful heart and a willing mind to use the gifts you are giving me."

There is no magic in the words we choose as opposed to words that you will use. The magic is in your faith.

PART TWO

The Value of Group Prayers

Circles of Prayer

It is time for groups of people to set up prayer and meditation meetings. They will meet to pray for the survival of mankind during the earth changes.

Pray for the upliftment of Man (here we refer to the totality of humanity and not to gender). Take prayer requests and pray for specific individuals.

Since we are calling you to serve under Mary, perhaps it would be good to review Her writings on prayer and meditation, and follow Her suggestions.

We have some suggestions which may parallel Hers or could provide you with new insight. Understand that you will take from these writings what rings true for you, and what clicks inside of you as truth.

The Format

As to how to hold and conduct these groups, each individual group will meet for the express purpose of prayer and meditation. The mechanics will not be as important as the intent. Let each group gravitate to those activities which seem right for its members. We urge each group to pray according to what is right for them.

Some may want to kneel or hold hands. Our preference is the holding of hands. The touching of hands with goodwill and good intent is a prayer. *The touching of hands in prayer allows energies which are unseen to flow and increase before going to the ethers to do as directed.*

Begin always with a moment of individual prayer, in which each person is allowed to forgive themselves and anyone else. Then forgive the world, all its inhabitants and all your ancestors, remembering that you are your ancestors.

Forgive governments, religions, and all institutions of man. Pour forgiveness into the race consciousness of mankind. Then bring love, wisdom, and truth into your being and allow it to flow into your home, city, state, continent, hemisphere, and then on to all the world.

Do this slowly, giving time for the idea to sink into your mind and heart. By connecting with Spirit, it is done. This is simply one way to pray for the world. *Everyone needs forgiveness; everyone needs love.* In order to radiate love, forgiveness must be a part of your make-up. By allowing forgiveness to be active in you, it is easy to send it to mankind.

The Content

Bring love into your being; daily radiate love to everyone, all the time.

Next concentrate on peace. *Make peace with yourself, your Creator, and your family, and then send peace into the world.*

Concentrate on those countries that are in the midst of war. They do more destruction to themselves and their nation than they do to anyone else. In this light, pray for Africa. This whole continent is in a state of war each day.

Small wars spring up within cities, families, tribes, and within countries, but we see that they fight themselves more than anyone else. Send peace to Asia, for within their sector are many who are in a warring mood.

Pray for these continents, not only to put down arms, but to put away attitudes of control, malice, and close-mindedness. Pray and send peace to the European continent, for there are many who are resentful and angry. Send peace to the Middle East, for there is much hatred in the hearts of men. Pray for the American continents, for upon these lands is much abuse of all kinds. This does not mean that such conditions are seen only in these specific areas; it means that all these conditions are prevalent in every nation of the world.

Make peace with yourself by accepting that you are always loved. God loves and accepts you just as you are today. As you come to accept yourself, you will find things to improve within yourself. The improvements will be from a standpoint of gentleness and love, not of fear or loss. Accept that you are here to learn and share. This is really all that is required at this time.

You are to forgive and love, first yourself and then your world, accepting that every event and situation in your life is for the express purpose of learning. You are always learning something, therefore you are always in motion.

Understand that the best you can ever do for people is to pray for them. Prayer is an outpouring of all the forces of the Universe for improvement. Prayer is a shifting of the future into higher and higher good. It is uplifting. Prayer caramelizes (sweetens) people, circumstances, and events with love and goodness.

Pray for the transformation that is taking place in each of you. Then pray for the transformation that is taking place in the world. Ask each person in the world to accept the transformation, as it is only Goodness, Truth, and Love entering this atmosphere.

Pray that all transformations take place in peace, with gentleness and love. This will minimize fear and anger. People are inherently feeling the changes, and there is a natural reaction to fear of the unknown. By praying specifically for the transformation to take place with gentleness and love, you have increased the vibrations in man's consciousness to open the door to Peace, Hope, and Love.

Allow these groups to remain fluid and flexible, changing the way the meetings are held or conducted as the group sees fit. You will know when to effect a change: it will be revealed to you.

Step out and serve; many are being called and few are responding. It is far easier to sit back and allow someone else to do the work. But the coming events are of such a great nature that it is now taking everyone's efforts to effect change.

The Power of Group Prayer

Come together to pray as a group. This will instill power into your life.

Remember that Jesus told you that where two or more were gathered together in His name, there He would be.

We know that you have not always stated that you were gathered together in Jesus' name, but it is the same, as you are seeking to know more about God. In searching for truth, from the standpoint of God and Divine knowledge, you have called on all the Divine forces to come into play.

Your gatherings are important to us and to many who are with you.

This has added strength to your family and to each of you individually. For a period of time, you have set aside the world to concentrate on the eternal.

As you pray, what you pray for is answered, for you have gathered a group of beings who are willing to help you pray and understand how this all works.

Divine Love and all of the Power of the Universe is around you, waiting only for you to activate it.

These meetings for prayer are being attended by many spirit beings, who are also concentrating on your efforts.

This helps to activate All of God's many attributes in your minds.

Prayer can be activated automatically, but there is power in the uniting of your prayers. For with a group as a unit, you have more power to turn the right knobs, or set the dial correctly, for the answers to your prayers.

It takes faith to receive what you ask for. At times, the faith of one alone may be weak, and one may find it difficult to maintain faith. But in a group unit there is strength. That is why it is good to unite in a church. It gives you the ability and strength of the group.

Let us use an analogy. Say you are one light bulb emitting light alone. There is light given off, but when you are joined by many light bulbs, what happens? There is much light, which can be seen even into the heavens.

When your astronauts were up in space once, there was a city that turned on its lights as they passed over, high in space. The city was so illuminated that it could be seen in space. This was Perth, Australia, remember?

As you unite to pray in a group, individually you are strengthened by the number and faith of your group.

Pray for the Good
of the Nation

We urge you to continue to pray for the good of this nation and for good leadership to guide the affairs of the world. This is your ability to help establish the truth in all things.

We urge you also to pray for your scientists to see the truth about this planet and to have a government which will act on these truths.

Pray that you will be prepared for the coming events and that your nation will see and prepare, but remember to pray for the world and all nations to prepare.

Pray for the World

We ask each person to make a list of the names of their loved ones and friends. List all people who are members of your earthly family, list all friends, and list all enemies. In this way you will be complying with Mary's wish for prayer for this world.

Start with your family and loved ones. Through love the connection will be made quickly. Through your love, which will connect to God's Love, your prayers will be answered so that the best outcome in each circumstance will be done.

Daily pray for all the people in the family prayer basket. Understand that only through prayer and in meditation will you grow spiritually. Only through spirit will your connection be made to All Good, which is God.

All people are one family on this earth planet. Therefore, as people come together to pray, they will become each a unit of spiritual family.

I request that you take seriously my request to help me pray for the world, as a planet, as a people, and as your home.

Prayer for Well-Being

*F*ather God, I request per Mother Mary's wish that you send your Love into the hearts and minds of all men, women, and children of this world. I ask that you forgive us all of our erroneous thoughts and beliefs. Forgive our ignorance, our mistakes in thinking there are many gods, when in reality there is only You, Father.

Help each of us on earth to open our eyes to the mistake we make in abusing our land, our minds, and our hearts. Help each of us as we seek to correct the conditions and thoughts that prevent us from seeing the Light, which is your Love.

Father God, help each of us to correct in our own lives those areas which need to be changed, to accept those parts of our lives which cannot be changed, but most of all Father God, give us the wisdom to see the difference.

We ask, Father God, as each of us works on himself, that this will help the collective consciousness of mankind. May this soon be the normal way of thinking, that mankind will think only of You and your Love.

Send your peace into the world and into those areas of the world that are torn apart with wars. Help each one to reflect Your Peace in his or her heart, mind, and life. I surrender all that I am to You, Father God. I surrender all that I hope to be and all I can be to your Love.

Thank you, Father God, for hearing my prayer and for your answer. Amen.

Pray for All Humanity

Pray that each person on earth will see with spiritual eyes the issues that are important.

Pray for all Mormons, Muslims, Jews, Hindus, Shintos, Buddhists, Catholics, Protestants, and all people. Pray for those who are agnostic and atheist, for those who follow their own way of seeking God.

There is but one God and one Heaven and one Spiritual Realm. All people will enter this realm sooner or later.

It is for this reason that I request your help in prayer, *because prayer is cumulative in nature, and all prayers help toward this end; each prayer is added to past prayers that you have said and that we have said.*

Pray daily, not only for yourself but for the cleansing of the minds of men, for the cleansing of the minds of governments, and of leaders of the world.

Group Meditation on Universal Light

Now, a suggestion for a group meditation. Take a globe and place it in the center of a circle of people. Open your hands palms out. Allow all the energy of the universe to flow through you into this representation of the world. In your mind's eye see light, love, and energy flowing from your hands into the world, each nation, and each ocean.

There is power in the coming together of those who seek daily to find their inner light. Your light shines more brightly when you share. This is how to share who and what you are.

Decide, commit, and then go into action. All is happening quickly now; it is time for this phase of the work to begin. We are available to you as inner guides or simply as assistants in your prayer circles.

We see each of the prayer circles as gears in a motor, moving the future toward Universal Light, Love, and All Goodness. As more prayer circles are formed, this creates a bigger motor to shift the future, world, and humanity toward The Source.

If you cannot set up a prayer circle at this time, then support one with your time and energy. Choose one of the circles that is closest to your home. Not everyone will set up prayer circles: many are needed as participants. Everyone is needed; everyone is important and has their own place in this plan. Everyone is loved greatly.

Quantum Time

Let us address the concept of time. Time has been in high gear for awhile. It has sped up, and you are in what is called "quantum time." This is a whole topic in itself. But allow us to say this: understand that since time is moving at a faster rate now, your prayers will effect change quickly.

Your meditations on Love raise the consciousness of mankind quickly. As you pray for humanity, more and more minds are opening to the possibility of a life beyond what is seen or felt. People are opening up to new ideas of life and the importance of life.

From now on, situations will become more difficult for everyone. People who rely on the Father within to provide, will find not only solace and comfort, but all their needs met.

If something is taken away from your life, understand that it isn't for your future. Allow Spirit to enter your mind and heart, changing your motives, concepts of yourself, ideas on service and ideas on what is needed. Ask Spirit to help you understand this fast-changing world and your part in it.

Begin to think about prayer circles and discuss ways to begin prayer and meditation circles: where will they be held? If not in your home, then where? when? what night or day?

Do not worry about who will come; when you have opened your homes and churches to prayer and meditation, people will find you. Decide when you will come together to discuss and share your joys, ideas, and inspirations.

Know that you will never be alone. Jesus promised that where two or three meet in his name, he will be there. This is his commitment to you who serve. The Brotherhood and many more who are praying for this world will be with you.

As you serve, you grow spiritually. This is the only growth that is necessary. You will find much coming from these circles: poems, prayers, healings, and stories. Keep a record of what is beautiful and useful to others in the way you prayed and of how it was successful.

Prayer is so wonderful because it is the shifting of circumstances and situations towards the Good.

If something negative or harmful (we like this word better) is in the future, through prayer you will shift it toward the Good.

When you pray for humanity's good, you will shift circumstances and situations quickly. This is above and beyond the quickness of quantum time. You will see results in a short time. I recommend praying for these circumstances:

1. For your own awareness of a continued inner connection to the Father.

2. For the good of your city: environment, politics, government, economics, social concerns, and the spiritual health of each citizen and all the animals. (You may add to this list.)

3. Then pray this same way for your nation.

4. Pray for the world in this manner. Include the oceans, forests, plains, and deserts.

5. Pray for the world's future and the population's future.

All future circumstances and situations are fluid.

The future can be changed through prayer, by moving it into the light of Good.

✦ ∘ ✦

Pray for Those
in Abuse and Denial

Pray for the minds of those people who are hiding their little addictions, and for those who openly abuse their bodies, to see the light. When the light of Truth has entered the minds of men, then they will not deny their habits.

Pray for the addict, for governments of the world, for family members of the addict, for the society of the world. Everyone is affected by this rampage of abuse. Every sector of society is harmed. Even those who do not have anything to do with drugs and alcohol, abuse the body with food, sex, work, or any habit that takes over one's life.

People can and do become addicted to their individual religions. When a person spends more time on matters of their individual religion instead of in prayer, that person is abusing his mind. It does not matter which religion has the most people in its churches or the most money. It does not matter the clothing or the fixtures of the church. What does matter is the Spirit of the religion. It is the Spirit of people that matters.

PART THREE

The Art of Meditation

Understand the Power
of Visualization

Visualization is handy in getting you into the right mind-set for your life. It will help you see results or solutions. This way you will be exercising your mind and spirit.

Allow your mind to dominate your life, because it does anyway. You live from a mental standpoint and not from a physical standpoint.

Yes, you must take care of the physical body, but this can be fun, if you allow it to be. Make games of caring for your body. Have fun living life. It not only is a school, but a pleasure too.

Understand that visualization is a tool to make your life easier. It will help to focus your mind on the end results and not on problems.

Remember, whatever your subconscious receives as your desire, that is what it will work towards. This is the danger in worry, because you give your subconscious the wrong idea of your desires. Through creating specific images, it gives your mind clear pictures and direction of what you desire.

Leave the end result and the unfolding plan to God-Mind. Allow Him to give you this or *something better!* Allow God to make the last decision as to what is best for you. This way you are able to release the solution to God-Mind. As you release and give it to God, He will be free to give back to you what is best.

Become still in the closet of your mind. *It is now time for you to use this stillness to communicate with God-Mind and to strengthen your ability to communicate.*

It is imperative that you learn to use your mind to get information and guidance. And in order to do this, you must strengthen the mind by using it. This is why we continually give you mental exercises to do.

From time to time it may be necessary for you to go off into a quiet place to commune with God, but for now this is your lesson. The lesson is to set up a good line of communication with God-Mind.

We urge you to follow Jesus' lead and example of going within to commune with God. You may want to go to a solitary place to pray. Read in the Bible and find all the passages that tell of how Jesus went alone to pray, as in Mark 1:35.

Even Jesus, who had the greatest connection to God-Mind, needed this quiet prayer time. You do too. Jesus was in constant, direct communication with God; at times even he found it necessary to go alone and pray.

Notice the time of day when Jesus went alone to pray. Most always it was during the night, early in the morning, or late at night. There is a reason for going alone in the night. During the day there is much activity in the world and this emits vibrations. Your very body is activated by the vibrations of all this activity. Most animals are day animals for this reason.

Each person has a magnetic field, and this acts like a magnet and is quickened by the activity of life. It causes your heart to beat a little faster, your breathing is a little quicker; all your reactions are hastened.

During the night, on the other hand, the pace is slowed down. The animals sense this and they become drowsy and will sleep. (Of course we are aware of the animals who have a reverse time clock and hunt at night.)

But notice the level of activity at night and how very quiet the world becomes. It is during this time that your magnetic field, reactions, even the autonomic part of your brain is turned down. It is much easier and more effective to communicate with Spirit.

Once in a while, try getting up during the night to pray and visualize. The results will be amazing.

This is your task for the coming year: to strengthen your ability to communicate with Spirit.

Visualizing Enlightenment

"And ye shall have dominion over them." We will use these words to give a good lesson. It is one that is true and well timed. What you have dominion over are your thoughts, words, actions, attitudes, all issues of your life. In the story of creation, it says, *". . . and they shall have dominion over the birds in the air and over the fishes in the ocean, over every living thing man will have dominion." (Gn 1:28)*

Now use your inner self and decipher these words. The birds of the air are your thoughts. The fishes of the sea are your attitudes, urges, perhaps even your addictions, those things you wish to or already keep secret or under cover.

The animals who roam the earth are your wandering thoughts, your wandering eye, or that which is within you that leads you astray.

Now this verse of the Bible simply says you will have dominion over every area of your life. So visualize all the good that you desire in your life, and begin with your spiritual life. Give it the importance it deserves.

In visualizing the increase of your spiritual life, use something like this: allow the bright sun to represent God-Mind, and see yourself sitting in a meadow or by the sea.

Next see the sunrays coming toward you. The sunrays will become an elevator and take you to the sun, which has represented God-Mind for ages. In the beginning of this visualization, give yourself *the intention of becoming one with God-Mind and all that God is.*

Do you have some area of your life that troubles you? Bring this area to the temple in your mind and pray about it. Is there some person who troubles you? Do the same. Is there something you have need of? Visualize the results you desire, but first take it into your temple and pray.

Prayer is your ability to communicate and speak to Father-God. Visualization is an exercise for your mind and heart to agree on the results you desire.

How to Meditate

Here is the "catch": use meditation to commune with God-Mind only. As you develop the ability to commune with God-Mind, your mental and psychic powers will be increased. They will evolve naturally.

Since your aim is to develop mentally and spiritually, we urge you to learn to visualize. Understand that each of you can become proficient in the use of this mental power. *What you can visualize and believe to be true will BECOME TRUE IN YOUR EXPERIENCE.*

We ask that you begin to use visualizations that we will place in your mind. Here are some simple rules to follow:

1. Always start your visualization with "the problem." That is, begin with what is bothering you.

If it is physical, like an earache, you will enter your body (mentally) through the ear, and begin to clean it out and use healing agents.

If your problem is finances, then you will enter your checkbook and ask what it is you need to "see." If you do not have a checkbook, then take your pay, as money, and build a house in your mind with the money. Enter the money and ask it to reveal what you need to know. Then sit inside the mental house or checkbook and become quiet.

Whatever you see, feel, or hear will reveal the problem to you. Arise, find a bucket filled with money in the corner of a room. Begin to take money and use it to add on to your house. As money is pulled from the bucket, more springs from the center of the bucket. Fill your rooms with this money, then sit down and sense the feeling of satisfaction. Then open your eyes.

2. Everything is possible in visualization. You will always find a way out, an aid or convenience.

If you find yourself in a well, there will be a ladder for you to use to climb out of the well. If you are in a dark place, light will come from the tips of your fingers. Do not analyze this process. Simply use whatever means are available to you through your visualizations.

3. If at first you think you are unable to visualize, then simply tell yourself this is happening in your mind. Remember, your mind will speak to you through every sense available. It will speak through your feelings, hearing, taste, sight, smell, or voice. As with all new lessons, it takes practice.

4. Use visualizations to see the completion of your goals. Simply see and sense how you will look, feel, smell, or be when this goal is completed.

5. Always sit in an upright position with feet comfortably on the floor. Take three or four normal breaths through your nose, and let them out through your mouth slowly. Then state your intention for the visualization or meditation.

Say to yourself, "My intention is to see my completed goals." Or, "I intend to learn from this earache, or this heartache, or this lack of money." Whatever your intention is, claim it in your mind.

This process will help to improve your meditations.

Begin each meditation with your intention. If your intention is to commune with God-Mind, then say it to yourself. If you have a need or a problem on which you wish to meditate, then state this intention.

Now comes HOPE. Hope, as we define it, is the expectancy of a positive answer. This is part of your visualization. Expect to find the right answer or to have the problem dissolved.

We would like for you to look at your last year's goals. Note which goals have been reached. Congratulate yourself and see the things you have accomplished. Add what you have accomplished that isn't on your list. Then review the list.

Receive Knowledge
Nonverbally

Another reason for meditation is to receive knowledge in a nonverbal way. True knowledge can be given to you non-verbally. It is mankind who needs words to describe everything. In spirit we have methods that are as elementary in nature as the amoeba. These are pure communication, in which words or terms are not needed.

That is why Jesus taught in stories and parables. He always started off by saying, "The kingdom of heaven is likened unto this." God in His Infinite Intelligence has many ways to give knowledge and understanding that do not require words. When you are able to quiet your mind, you can receive knowledge, wisdom, know-how, practicality, and many more things in total that will help you with your life goals.

At first you may envision knowledge, understanding, all the good God has to give, as a stream of Light that enters the head. Be aware that something is transpiring in and around your body.

Set up, as a goal in meditation, the ability to communicate with God in nonverbal terms, simply to sense the Love and Understanding which God gives happily. As you persist, God is more and more joyful, and so are we. As each of you seeks God in your heart and mind, we in spirit are joyful, for we have the assurance that you will get the results you desire—that is, if your desires do not in any way harm anyone. At times you can simply sit and tell your mind and heart to communicate with God in nonverbal terms. Then bask in the Love that is yours and everyone's.

How to Meditate on Goals

The setting of goals is the first step. If you have not done this, do it fast. It is a waste of time and energy to live one day without a goal. This is a form of abuse, abuse of time and energy.

Look to every area of your life: spiritual, physical, emotional, mental, family, career, and recreational. Perhaps some of your goals cannot be accomplished in this year. There may be steps to take this year, to progress to the completion of the goal.

For instance, as a student, one of the goals could be the completion of education for a career. It will not happen in one year, but as the student works and looks forward to the completion of the goal, they progress.

In other areas, look to the completion of the goal, no matter how long it takes.

Another example could be a desire to become better parents. This is a task that will take a lifetime. It demands flexibility and honesty. It demands much love and compassion. It is not a goal that is completed in one year, but keep a log of this goal, and see how much better your relationship with your children grows.

Now, the second step is in focusing your concentration. When you can focus on a desired result, you will see the completion and the reward. It takes a focus of concentration in order to complete any task, but more so to keep the interest in your life.

As an example, when you look into a pair of binoculars and they are not focused, what do you see? Blurred visions, half sights, these are the things you see. But as you focus the binoculars, you see clearly and are able to find the desired sight. Likewise, a life without a goal is a blurred vision. If you cannot focus on one goal, there is no hope of accomplishment; everything is possible and nothing is accomplished.

It is true that everything is possible, but without a focus or a goal, nothing will be accomplished. As you focus on your goals this year, you will be better able to focus on a completion, or on the progress to a completion.

Third is prayer. Without prayer you will have a difficult time completing your goals. With prayer, ideas will enter your mind to make the task easy. Knowledge will come to the forefront, and you will simply know how to do, or what to do.

Prayer answers in ways that are not always visible to you. Prayer can put you in the right place at the right time. You can find a search shortened for an item that is necessary for your progress. Prayer relieves your mind of stresses that are unimportant. Prayer will give you the know-how and the power to find the way to complete your goals.

When you release your goals in prayer to God-Energy, you are using the Greatest Power in the Universe. You feel the satisfaction of knowing you are in line with your Spirit-self.

Continue to pray daily. Have faith in God the Father, but be aware that we are also using the Whole Spirit and Essence of God to pray with you and to pray for those people whom you love. The network consists of you, the Brotherhood, me, and God. You are using the Whole of God-Essence in this manner. You are using the Trinity.

View this Trinity as a pyramid, with yourself standing inside it. There is a spiritual significance to the pyramid. By using this vision, you will be healed and progress faster. In your meditations use this vision. In old Egypt a triangle was used, with an eye in the center representing the individual. This is you in perfect harmony with all of God's Creation.

You are continuously in this Trinity.

How to Unblock
Your Circumstances

Allow an analogy. God is secure and stable as a very large tree. Upon this tree hang several ribbons. We will say in this analogy that the tree represents God as the One Secure and Stable element in your life. You, as people, are represented by the different ribbons. The wind is the circumstances of your life. When the winds of circumstance blow gently, then you as the ribbon are slightly moved. But when the wind of life's circumstances blows with more force, you become entangled by the winds and a blockage and a twisting occurs.

We could say this twisting and blockage of the ribbons happens in your life. As the winds of life's circumstances blow through your life, you will be able to use the very same wind to become disentangled. But always the tree remains secure and safe, a refuge and a rock in time of trouble.

To unblock the mental concepts that are keeping you from your full potential, you must become One, united with the security of God-Essence. Use the circumstances in your life to remove all tangled thoughts. *Use your life just as it is now to become One with God and All He Is.*

Stating "I Am"
for Full Potency

It is through the words "I AM" that you are connected to God. Whatever you say after "I AM" becomes truth. Watch your words, your thoughts, and especially your feelings. This is how to bring your expectations up to the top level, to your full potential and capacity.

Be careful of the words that follow "I AM." If you say, "I am tired," you are bringing this condition into your life. If you say, *I am provided for by God,* this is a Spiritual truth and will quickly manifest in your life, as soon as you truly believe the words with feeling.

✥ ○ ✥

Ask for Your Hidden Blessings

Look at every situation in your life and ask it to bless you. Every circumstance has a lesson for you only. It is how you react to life that determines how you live life, no matter what the situation is or whom the event has affected most.

If you are involved, there is a lesson for you. There is a hidden blessing for you! The blessing is in learning the lesson.

Ask the situation to give you information. Then become quiet in your mind and allow pictures, words, or thoughts to enter. You will find in this way that you can learn your lessons easily and quickly. Direct the events in your life now. Find the key to your blessing.

There is good for you in every event in your life, no matter how dark or dire the circumstance.

Perhaps it is in releasing an emotion that you no longer need. Perhaps it is in forgiving yourself or someone else. There is a mental act or an emotional deed that needs to be performed in every situation.

The Steps
to Entering God-Mind

Have faith that you are in God-Mind consciousness when you have done the next steps. Remind yourself that your feelings may not be telling you the truth.

The steps to entering God-Mind daily are:

1. *Meditate.* Enter your temple and request that you be connected to God-Mind. Have some symbol that will signify to your mind that you are in God-Mind; for some people it is a great, brilliant light coming from above. It could be music, or a special place in the temple that you enter to denote the entering of God-Mind consciousness.

Tell yourself that you will go about your daily activities, but that it will be from the standpoint of God-Mind consciousness.

Allow Divine Love to enter your being. There place any concerns to be worked out in Spirit, then awaken.

2. *Pray for the state of God-Mind consciousness.* Request with all your heart and mind to enter this Supreme Consciousness with ease. The request must be sincere and with earnestness. Then go about your daily activities.

3. Throughout the day, *affirm that you are in God-Mind consciousness* no matter what you are feeling. In this state of mind you are connected to the Source of all Good.

Affirm that your needs are being met in an orderly fashion, and at the right time they will appear in your life. Affirm positively that no matter what is occurring in your life, it will improve as you remain in God-Mind consciousness.

4. *Throughout the day, be grateful to God-Mind.* Simply say, "Thank you Father, for the ability to enter your Great Mind and live this day from the perspective of Spirit."

5. *Remain faithful to these exercises.* Do them daily, either in the evening or in the morning, whichever is convenient for you. If you do your meditation in the evening for the next day, you will simply say, "For the next 24 hours, as you enter your meditation.

To remain faithful to your course, affirm the following or something similar:

"I live in God-Mind and do not worry or concern myself with exterior events, no matter how pressing the need. In God-Mind I am completely taken care of: all my needs are being met at the right time and in the right manner."

It will be through this connection that every person will receive their own instruction. You will not fear anything or any event in the future, because you are in the ultimate state, and you will, in this reality, begin to enter the consciousness that gives access to your full potential.

Use Love to
Heal and Forgive

Divine Love and all love is much, much more than a feeling. It is an energy like electricity.

Use Divine Love to heal bodies, relationships, finances, business, nations, and the planet.

Concentrate on Divine Love and visualize the person who needs a healing. In this manner you are asking Divine Love, which is God the Father, to heal this person.

There is no need to plead or beg, you have the ability to use your mind and heart as did Jesus in prayer. Jesus said at the end of his petition, "Thank you, Father, because you have heard me." He was sure of God's ability to hear him, because he was aware of this inner connection to God's Love.

You can heal the family by stating that Divine Love is flowing through you to all whom you love.

Use love to forgive, first yourself and then others.

As you forgive everyone in this lifetime, you are forgiving all the residue of past lives. It is good to forgive all people and all events of past lives, because *you stop the wheel of karma by forgiving.*

When you first begin to forgive past lives, there may be a short period of pain in which the memory cells are emptied. But continue to forgive, and soon there is a release as there has never been in your life.

Meditation to Quiet the Mind

To meditate, this is what you must do. Find a moment that will allow you to quiet your mind. Become dreamy, in a half-awake and half-asleep mood. This is the meditative mood you are looking for.

Picture in your mind a most peaceful place. Perhaps it's the seaside, or mountains, or your backyard. It does not matter where this place is; it is the mood of the place that is important.

Continue to feel this half-asleep mood. Picture your dreams about the life that would be your ideal. Then stop all thoughts and simply feel Light as it pours into your head. Stay as quiet in your mind as you can, for as long as you can.

Allow God one split second to pour knowledge and understanding into your mind. You can help Him do this by thinking, "As I blank my mind, God is pouring in knowledge, understanding, and wisdom."

Then blank your mind as best you can. Try this for one week.

Bask in the Light of God

This is the method to wait on the Lord: In the quietness of your being, imagine God as a Light, which He is, pouring into your head, filling your heart with His Being. Sit and bask in this wonderful Light. Feel the unconditional love as it infiltrates every cell and every thought. In this manner, you open yourself to God and to All God Is.

Now, in this week, practice this meditation. You will receive instruction, gifts, and an opening to more of yourself through meditation. While communing with God-Mind and God-Father, you will be filled to overflowing with All that God is—Energy, Love, Forgiveness, Hope, Peace, and Power. These are simply a beginning of the ways to identify God in your heart and mind.

The White Bubble of Light

Become quiet, by holding your body still for one minute, while having a sense of a draining away of tensions quickly. Tell yourself the following or some words to this effect:

"I place myself in a white bubble of Light, which to my mind represents God-Mind consciousness. The outer layer of this light acts as a membrane, in that it allows into my mind only those truths I need today. On the other hand, it acts as a vacuum cleaner and removes instantly any thought or feeling that is not truth. God now surrounds me with His good. I am Divinely protected, Divinely guided, and Divinely successful today."

Then go about your day in confidence and love. If during the day you find yourself becoming tense and frustrated, simply enter into your short meditation of the morning and the idea of this great bubble of Light. Remind yourself of the wonderful love that comes to you daily from us, Jesus, Mary, and, most important, from God.

The Balloon Meditation

Simply *meditate by concentrating on the words hope, peace, and love.* As you send out these thoughts of love, peace, and hope, think of them as balloons filled with these essences. See these balloons of peace, love, and hope going through the air to all parts of the world. Send these thoughts to people, oceans, rivers, animals, mountains, and to plains. You could easily spend much time with this one method of prayer.

$\rightarrow \circ \leftarrow$

A Simple Way
to Build Inner Power

This is an example of how to use energy. Upon awaking in the morning allow five minutes to make contact with the Power of God within. Simply say to yourself, *"Today I choose to live in the Energy of God the Father."* Then pray your morning prayer. This will set your mind in the direction of the Father within.

Arise and stretch your body as you stretch your mind toward Good. Take time out at intervals to monitor your attitude and words. Perhaps when there is a lull, ask, "Have I been using the thoughts and words that represent the conditions I want in my future?"

With your noon meal take a quick moment to think, *"I will stay in contact with the Giver of Life."* Before retiring for the night, write about your day, and include the events that you want to be rid of.

Perhaps it was an unusually good day and you are grateful. Or perhaps there was some dissension and you need to forgive. When you forgive, all you do is *give up* the resentment, fear, or other depleting emotion and *give a* word of encouragement. You will face your new day free of all past regrets, fears, and depleting emotions.

The reason we refer to negative emotions as depleting is because they continuously drain energy, as opposed to the lighter emotions, which continuously give you energy such as love, peace, and happiness.

Daily Meditation
and Prayer Program

Here is how we recommend that you meditate and pray.

Set a separate time for meditation and one for prayer. Perhaps it can be that you meditate early in the morning or you pray early in the morning.

Use a meditation to begin your day. In meditation you will first still the body; you may find this easier in the early morning or late at night. State what your meditation will be concentrating on.

Meditate on one thought, such as peace, health, love, wisdom, or understanding. Your meditation need not be long time-wise, but it must be unhurried. Use your imagination to cleanse all negativity from your mind. Do this quickly with words and with an image of light.

We recommend that you *sit upright to meditate,* to prevent you from falling asleep. Visualize a green cleansing light, or use the color of your choice, but afterwards always use this color for cleansing.

Stand in a circle of this color of light and think, *"I am being cleansed of all negative thoughts, fear, anger, and hidden resentments. As I am cleansed I forgive all people, and all people forgive me. It is done, it is accomplished."*

Silence all thoughts and then mentally stand in a circle of white light to be healed, protected, and guided for the day. Repeat the word for this day. The word in this case could be Forgive, Peace, Cleansed, Love, Accomplish, or Blessings.

Remain in the state of meditation for a few minutes. Then awaken with the thought of feeling energetic and ready to meet all the activity of the day. This will not take long. It is an exercise of the mind to cleanse and heal.

Throughout the day, as people come to mind, forgive them and say the word of the day as a prayer for them. If for instance you are using the concept of PEACE, then you will bless everyone you meet with peace in your heart, in your mind, and immersed in your aura. If the word is LOVE, then do the same. You can say, "I send PEACE to you and forgive you of all transgressions.

End all meditations with a short prayer for the day. Say something like, "Father, please be with me today and bless all the people I see." Or, "Father, give me the strength to find peace in my heart and in the faces of others. Use the word for the day as a prayer.

Set a time in the evening for prayer. *Be faithful to this time, and pray daily in this manner.*

First, you will ask that all thoughts, deeds, and attitudes be forgiven in you and in those for whom you pray. Then pray for your loved ones, and be specific at this time as to how you perceive their needs. Realize that God sees All and knows All.

Then pray for the people with whom you work, you play or meet. Pray for areas of the world by continents and by religions. Pray for those who do not believe in God the Father, that they may be enlightened.

Weekly change the way you pray, so that it will not become rote and lose its meaning. Also change the place you pray: sometimes use the outdoors and sit in nature to pray. At other times you may want to drive to a lake or pond of water to pray. Pray in a different room, change the clothes you wear or the locale, but *do not change the time*. Remain constant in this and see your faith increased.

PART FOUR

Developing
Your Inner Divinity

Meditations
on the Energy Centers

Meditate daily on each energy center (corresponding to the major chakras in the body), and then concentrate on the energy that is needed. *If you are feeling unloved, then concentrate on the center of Love and allow all this word means to conjure ideas or thoughts to heal you.* It will not happen in one meditation, but with time it will come about. Be patient and persistent, and it will pay off in great benefits.

Meditate on these energies and remember that it is for your good and not ours that you meditate. Our aim is to help by bolstering and supporting your efforts to connect to the Father within.

The First Center:
Life and Strength

The center of life brings the ability to change and adapt. Use this energy when you are faced with changes that need to take place. If there is a change in jobs, you will call upon life energy to help adapt and adjust to new people and new routines.

If there is a move of residence, you will call upon life and strength to aid in all adjustments to environment, climate, home, people, and routines.

Where there is life, there is activity, an ability to adapt to surroundings and differing conditions.

Think of strength. These are some of the words that describe strength: courage, might, force to withstand, an ability to support, vigor, firmness, potency.

Strength as we use it is the ability to last, endure, and the capacity to perform.

Use Strength for the ability to endure when you are faced with something that is out of your control.

Or use Strength for the potency to work and act in an effective manner, such as when you need to make changes in habits or thought patterns.

The Second Center:
Divine Order and Harmony

The second center is Order. *Divine Order is the highest and best order possible, anytime or anyplace.*

Words to describe order are: an authority, control, choice, status, harmony. It is the ability to have things in their proper place, to command, supply, regulate, conduct, and manage. It is the same order that holds the planets in their proper orbits. It is alignment in its proper perspective.

The center for Order is the same Universal Order of the planets. When you feel disharmony or find yourself in a condition that seems unmanageable, *Divine Order is the energy that can help you find harmony and the ability to cope.* This is your ability to command your attitudes, beliefs, and habits.

This opens up the energy to harmonize, to take the authority to choose. You have the innate ability to manage and regulate your life already, but perhaps it has been depleted through concentrating on the wrong emotions.

As Divine Order is brought into play in each life, there is stability, harmony, and peace, which inhabits all aspects

111

of life. One part of your life will not overpower the others. You have time to work, play, and to pray and meditate. You are free to choose, manage, and regulate your own life.

As you call forth the energy of Divine Order into all parts of your life, it brings about a harmony of its own. Evoke Divine order into your marriage, relationships, career, finances, even into your choices of what to buy.

When you bring into your mind the thought of Divine Order, it will protect you, allow more self-control and give you a feeling of status.

⤙ ° ⤚

The Third Center:
Wisdom and Knowledge

Wisdom and Knowledge are located in the pit of the stomach. This is your ability to sense the Truth. It is often called "gut feeling.: When you open this energy center, you will have the ability to judge properly and take action when needed.

Knowledge gives you the ability to use spiritual Truths and Divine Intelligence. This is the seat of common sense and the ability to know. When faced with the need to recall certain facts, use this inner energy center. When faced with questions about beliefs or attitudes, you will know how and what to say.

All the Knowledge in the Universe is within you, in this energy center. It is through this energy center that every person will receive their own instruction.

＊ ∘ ＊

The Fourth Center:
Love and Will

The next center is the center of Love and Will. Love is forgiveness. To love is to forgive until the number seven plays out. You forgive, forever and ever. You forgive all people and, most important, forgive yourself. This is the essence of love.

Love is tolerant, adoring, loyal, and freeing. When you truly love, you release and give up all control. Love is never inhibiting or selfish. You have many feelings and thoughts of love, but understand that *Divine Love is not controlling or manipulative.* It is used only with the highest and best results. Allow this unconditional Love to invade your inner life. God is always loving each of you, even when you do not feel it.

Diine Will is the ability to choose, deliberate, take action. It is purpose, determination, and persistence.

It is your Divine right to choose all situations in your life. If you do not choose, you are left to the effects of the past or to karma. *The best course of action is to will to do God's Will,* because God's Will is always good. God wants you to be as successful as you desire to be. He wants you to be healthy, wealthy, happy, and satisfied with your life.

It is in aligning to God's Will that you find shortcuts to these states of mind. Pray to have God's Will active in your life. Say often, *I will to do God's Will."* Or, *God's Will for me is only good, so I choose to have His Will active in my life."*

The Fifth Center:
Power and Enthusiasm

Zeal is enthusiasm, diligence, interest, eagerness, ardor, and avidity. Daily call upon Divine Enthusiasm to flow through you to increase your power to move, act, and be effective. All these energy centers are interconnected and flow one into the other.

When you are lacking in zeal, you are lacking in life, power, and love. If you must start with only one energy center, start with zeal. It's the most readily available. It will demonstrate the proof people need of the existence of these centers of energy.

The Sixth Center:
Imagination and Understanding

The third eye has always been magical. It is the seat of Imagination and Understanding.

Understanding is the ability to perceive the meaning of any situation, the ability to grasp ideas from Universal consciousness, to comprehend, realize, believe, and use all intellectual faculties.

Imagination is the most exciting of all energies, because it gives you the ability to paint pictures of your future. Remember to leave everything up to God to give what you picture or better. Through this energy center is the ability to see yourself as God sees you—beautiful, energetic, filled with enthusiasm, kind, loving, understanding, powerful, forgiving, wise, knowledgeable, alive, strong, intelligent, and successful.

Quiet your mind by breathing out three times. That is, concentrate on the breathing out and relaxing during the out breath. Then fill your imagination with pictures of the life you desire. Next, release these to God's Divine Will. This is how to use this magical center of energy.

You can also use imagination for your loved ones by simply saying in your meditation, "I see you as God sees you," and then list all these qualities. This is a very powerful prayer.

Use your imagination to paint the pictures of life. When you desire to have new friends, rejoice in your imagination with them. When you need a new work experience, see yourself coming home tired and happy from your new job. *See the results, the finished picture.* Or, better yet, see yourself banking the money you earned from the new job. Let this be your prayer.

Use your imagination to see peace in the world. Use this faculty to see headlines in your newspaper of *PEACE* in large bold letters. When you need a healing of the physical body, see yourself (in meditation) enjoying perfect health, doing the things you would do if you were well, playing games with family and friends.

Or, if you need anything, see (in your imagination) the thing completed or done, not the process but the completion of the request. Leave the process completely up to God the Father.

The Seventh Center: Spiritual Awareness

The most important energy center is the Spiritual. This is the seat of your connection to God. It is at the top of your head. Spiritual in your language means vital principle, breath of life, conscious incorporeal being, supernatural, brave vigor, the essence or active principle, idealism.

But you know that *spiritual means All that is God, all that is known and all that remains unknown.* You are more alive in spirit than on earth. You are alive for eternity. This is your connection to Divine Potential.

By concentrating on the spiritual center of energy, you enhance all energy centers, because they all are interconnected and interdependent, the same way all things on earth are interconnected and interdependent. If you will simply look at nature and the laws of ecology, you will see evidence of this.

Not only is there an ecology of the natural planetary world, but there is an ecology of spirit. The ways of earth are also spiritual. The natural world simply reflects the spirit world.

The Spiritual center is your connection to the REAL World; it is your ability to use all that you are, to enhance your life on earth. By concentrating on this center, you activate all of God, as Principle, in your life.

You DO NOT need to know the exact manner this is activated. What you desire are the results. This will happen as you bring spiritual energy into your mind, body, and affairs.

If there is a lack of time to meditate, concentrate on the Spiritual center and allow it to activate all centers within you. Then go in peace and "know" that deep within is all that you need to face any situation in life. See inwardly and feel the spiritual center shower your entire body with its energy.

Energy is the substance of God Himself. The Father used Himself to create life, worlds, and universes. There is the ability, through life-energy, to adapt and change.

Concentrate on the Spirit of God

We pray that you will heed our teachings and use the lessons to open these energy centers daily. This will help every person open to the Father within, hear His instruction, and receive all the good He has prepared for you. *These lessons do you the maximum good only if you practice them.*

In this manner, allow the mind to bring what the words of the different energy centers mean to you, individually.

What does it mean to have Divine Will working in you, or to have all the Wisdom of the universe at your disposal? What does it mean to you to be Powerful and full of Zeal and Enthusiasm? How would you feel and act if you had all the Understanding of the Universe and all the Imagination? How do you feel when you concentrate on the top of your head with the thought, "Spirit of God?"

These are the energies that are already active within each person. They can become filmy and depleted as the person concentrates more on hostilities, angers, envies, and jealousies. When you wallow in self-pity and despair, you only deplete your own energies. It is not that God is

121

punishing you, instead it is that you are punishing yourself by what you concentrate on.

During your meditations, concentrate on the different energy centers. Take the knowledge within you and use it to increase these energies.

Our Message to You

Allow time for daily meditation and prayer. Learn to rely on the Father within for all your needs. He is loving you with a love and interest greater than any in this world.

Keep your focus on prayer and meditation, then all things will be added to you. This is Jesus' promise to the world. He said, "Seek ye first the kingdom of God, and all things will be added unto you." (Mt 6:33) This means to put first things first.

Begin by seeking the Father within. Then all the events, circumstances, and situations in your life will be improved. It would be good to read this entire sermon of Jesus' as it also includes The Lord's Prayer and much, much more of what we have been teaching.

God works through you and the situations of your life.

As you change inside, the events of your life change dramatically.

All You Need Is Within You

Expect these changes to bring you good, as only God gives. *Remember that God is all Love, Pure raw Energy, and He is non-judgmental. He loves because He sees the perfection in everyone.*

What appear as setbacks are in reality evolutionary changes. When old issues come into your life again and again, there is something for you to resolve and/or forgive.

If you feel that you are on a treadmill going nowhere fast, recall that there is something or someone who needs to be forgiven. Forgive fate or destiny, if that is how you view it. Forgive yourself for making mistakes. Forgive the ones who instigated the changes that are occurring in your life.

When you feel like fighting something, or that you are in a fight, realize that the fight is within you, and look there for the issue.

Some people are facing issues that are ancient and need resolving in order for them to rest in the eternalness of God.

Realize that all you need is within you, because all you need is God. This is not just a saying, but Truth. Trust that as you rely on God the Father, He will not allow you to come to any real harm.

Put These Ideas into Practice

Once again, we urge you to pray for the working out of all events. Pray, knowing that all you need is now in place. Pray that each person will find their direction with ease, clarity, and honesty.

How this works out in your life is through God's joy. He will put a plan into place, at the right time.

All you need for the future, He provides, if you will just believe and trust. Belief and trust are your currency in Spirit. Let each person put into practice these ideas. Allow yourself to become comfortable with this procedure of praying, understanding always that Spirit is fluid.

New ideas and methods will blossom. Bring all new ideas to share with each other. Share today what has worked for you in the past. Make a commitment to pray for Light, Love, and Peace to all men this day.

The Greatness of God

All your imagination and mind could never conceive the wonder and greatness of God the Creator. He is more wonderful, loving, giving, and powerful than anyone can imagine.

You are loved with a love that is greater than anything on earth. God is the love and the act of loving. He dearly loves you with a love that is all-encompassing and healing.

God loves me, now, just as I am. Simply to allow this love to encompass all that you are and all that you desire will be healing. God does not judge; He loves.

"Love the Lord God with all your heart, all your mind, and all your soul, and love your neighbor as yourself." (Mt 22:37, 39; Mk 12:30-31; Lk 10:27) This is your true purpose.

APPENDICES

How to Meditate for the Spiritually Dense

Byron Kirkwood

Have you ever said or thought, "I can't meditate?" I have. And I've heard quite a few others tell me that they have trouble meditating. Well, if you are in this category, this article is for you. If you can already meditate, then this article is not for you—don't waste your time reading it (unless you want to help someone who "can't meditate").

Learning to meditate to be able to receive guidance, to know what to do, or where to go, may be very important in the future as spiritual preparation for survival.

I am really amazed and envious at how Annie and others can experience such beautiful and imaginative meditations.

Mother Mary has told us that there are as many ways to pray as there are people. Along this line, I believe there are also as many ways to meditate. What I want to convey in this short article is what works for me—how I meditate. It may not be the "right" way for you, but it works for me.

In *Mary's Message* we are taught that prayer is "talking to God" and that meditating is "listening to God." What I've learned since is that *God talks to us in silence.* He can, if we let him, place thoughts and ideas in our mind that will be available to us later when we need them. Have you ever been asked a question, answered, and then wondered, "How did I know that?" This might be an example of thoughts that were placed in your mind prior to you needing them and used when you answered the question. This recognition that God can talk with us in silence is a *key factor* in me accepting my form of meditation.

When I give talks on being prepared, I normally explain that "I'm a Taurus, very grounded and tied to the earth"—and I feel somewhat "spiritually dense." So for me to understand things, they have to be "logical" or "practical." The key factors I mention in this article allow me to accept my ability to meditate as logical and practical.

In her talks, Annie often discusses meditating. She tells on me when she says that, "Sometimes when Byron's meditating . . . he snores." This usually gets a good laugh from the audience. She then explains that when she asked Mother Mary about this, she was told, "Let him meditate however is his way."

This is how I normally meditate. I go into my bedroom and close the door. I turn the air conditioner fan switch to the "on" position to obtain a continuous uninterrupted air flow. I turn my stereo on and put in an audio tape that has sounds of rain and a mild thunderstorm. I find this very relaxing. I sit in my comfortable recliner chair in the reclined position and cover up with a light blanket.

Then I state my intention that I am going to meditate. This is normally done just in my mind, but it can also be outloud. *This "stating your intention to meditate" is the second key factor in my meditating.* Often I say (in my mind or outloud), "I am going to meditate," or I may say, "I want to commune with God-Mind to strengthen my God-Mind connection." Or if I'm working on a problem, I may state, "I am going to meditate on _____," and mentally state the subject that I want to receive help with through meditation.

Then I get comfortable and relax, taking a few deep breaths and letting my mind clear. I find that I tend to put my hands above my head, interconnecting my fingers. I may rest my hands on the top of my head, or above my head, resting on the back of my recliner. I don't know why I do this, it just feels right for me. During the meditation I may lower my hands to my lap if I get uncomfortable.

When I first start the meditation, my mind is often full of garbage and concerns of the day. Don't fight these thoughts, just let them happen. If you try to block them, you usually wind up concentrating on them. When I'm at this point, I just listen to the sounds of the rain and imagine that I'm sitting out on a old cabin porch watching the rain come down in a beautiful country forest. I think this picture may be from a past lifetime, because it feels so real to me, as if it really happened.

Not blocking these first thoughts and letting them just flow through my mind is the *third key* to my meditating.

Usually at this point I begin to feel myself relaxing as my body enters that almost hypnotic state and feels sort of dull and tingling. Then often I don't remember anything else until I wake up and my audio tape is no longer going. My meditations usually last about 30 minutes. Although they are sometimes shorter, I seem to get what I need out of the meditation. Or they can be longer, especially when I'm tired and my body has rested during the meditation.

That's a normal meditation for me, although they vary depending on what I need to receive. The keys to this working for me are that I realize that I can receive information in silence, that I stated my intention to meditate before I take my (almost) nap, and I don't fight to block out the thoughts that enter my busy mind at the beginning of the meditation.

Above, I mentioned working on something and taking the question or problem into meditation. One example of this is when people ask us, "What's a safe area?" in regard to Earth changes. I first tell them about the maps that are available showing how the United States may look after the changes have been completed. Then I suggest that ultimately they have to determine what is "right" for them and their family. I suggest that they take this question into meditation and receive their own answer.

Also, when I was working on this article, I meditated first. In this case I had a small tape recorder handy and did not use my meditation tape. I just got quiet and relaxed.

When I got something for the article, I spoke it into the recorder. Then I would relax again and forget about everything until my next thoughts arrived.

I've found that if I try to force the thoughts that I want or need, as in the case of this article, I block them—I'm trying too hard. So I just relax and let whatever comes to me happen. The thoughts I'm looking for are the ones below the surface of my consciousness. These thoughts remind me of air bubbles rising to the surface of the water. The thoughts I'm trying to force remind me of a hard cover over the top of the water blocking the air bubbles from reaching the top. So I relax and let the deep thoughts come to the surface and reveal themselves to me.

Sometimes when starting my meditation, I imagine that the top of my head has two large doors that open upward to let God's light come into my mind. I "see" these doors opening into space and light shining in. This is my way of mentally opening my mind to God's communications with me.

Once in the past, I was looking for a piece of paper that I'd filed that a friend needed. I tried to remember where I'd put it to no avail. So I went into meditation with the intent of finding the lost document. I took my meditation nap and when I arose, I knew where it was. I got up and went directly to where I had filed the paper. The location had "bubbled up" from my consciousness.

It may help if you set a regular time of day to meditate—mine's usually after my noonday meal. And select a quiet place to meditate—as I mentioned, mine's in my bedroom in my recliner. If you travel, you will have to adjust your time and place, and that's okay.

There are also guided meditation tapes available to help you, such as the "Journey Within" by Connie Cornwell and Tim Caffee (available through B&A).

I don't know if this will help you or not, but it works for me. Hopefully by reading this you may get a few new ideas to help you meditate.

God Loves Me, Just as I Am!

As I kneel at the altar in prayer, God loves me.
If I'm sitting in a jail cell, God loves me.
As I'm caring for the sick, God loves me.
If I'm out robbing and stealing, God loves me.
When I'm happy, God loves me.
When I'm sad, God loves me.
When I'm angry and loud, God loves me.
When I'm calm and serene, God loves me.
When I'm abused, God loves me.
As I'm abusive to others, God loves me.
If I'm in bed with a disease, God loves me.
When I'm healthy and fit, God loves me.
If I'm poor, God loves me.
If I'm out of work, God loves me.
When I'm earning large sums of money, God loves me.
When I'm winning in life, God loves me.
When I think I'm losing, God loves me.
When I'm frustrated and resentful, God loves me.
As I remain in a state of prayer, God loves me.
When I'm depressed and feeling low, God loves me.
When I'm in a good mood, God loves me.

No matter where I am—or who I am—or how I am—or what I am——God loves me with a love that is
immeasurable and unlimited.

I AM LOVED, JUST AS I AM!

by Annie Kirkwood

Reference Table

To help you find the passages in *Messages to Our Family* corresponding to the sections in *Instructions for the Soul*, the following table shows the contents of *Instructions for the Soul* followed by the date the information was originally received as presented in *Messages to Our Family*.

Biography

Annie and Byron Kirkwood were married in 1985. They have a blended family composed of five sons, two daughters-in-law, and two grandsons. Annie is the author of *Mary's Message to the World* and *Mary's Message of Hope*. Byron is the author of the *Survival Guide for the New Millennium*. Their book, *Messages to Our Family* from which *Instructions for the Soul* has been compiled, contains the full text of the messages sent by the Brotherhood of God, Mother Mary and Jesus to Annie through her mind over a six-year period. These messages were sent as a "lesson" for their weekly prayer and meditation family group meeting.

Annie was previously a nurse (LVN), enjoys playing the piano and occasionally painting. She is still receiving messages.

Byron has an MBA from Southern Methodist University and was previously employed in the microcomputer and electronics industries.

Together they publish a bimonthly newsletter, travel giving talks and workshops, and have started their own mail-order business, B&A Products, providing products for spiritual advancement and emergency preparedness.

For a free sample or subscription information to
Mary's Message/Newsletter, write, fax, or call:

Mary's Message / Newsletter
Annie Kirkwood
Route 1 Box 100
Bunch, OK 74931-9705
Phone: (918) 696-5998 • FAX (918) 696-5999

THE SEQUEL TO MARY'S MESSAGE TO THE WORLD,
An inspiring new book of messages from Mother Mary

Mary's Message of Hope
Annie Kirkwood

Many people have been asking if Mother Mary continues to speak to Annie, and if there are further messages. Yes, She does, and there are many more messages. After *Mary's Message* was published, Mother Mary urged Annie to begin a bi-monthly newsletter to keep in touch with all Her readers. So now, after 26 issues, Annie has collected together all the messages given by Mother Mary since April 1992, which include updates to predictions and many new revelations.

ISBN: 0-931892-35-X,
144 pp., paper, $10.95

*"Dear children, pray without ceasing.
Do this always, sending thoughts of love and hope to all people of the world.
Think of those who have lost hope and do not feel love."*
—Mother Mary

"Through these messages many have found the love that She has for all of us. She truly instructs with gentleness, gives us comfort, and above all fills our hearts with hope."
—Annie Kirkwood

Messages to Our Family

From the Brotherhood, Mother Mary, and Jesus

Annie and Byron Kirkwood

"This material may equal A Course in Miracles in finding its way into the hearts and minds of many. It provides spiritual food to nourish the journey through daily life." —Carol E. Parrish-Harra, Sparrow Hawk Village

ISBN: 0-931892-81-3,
540 pp., $17.95

This most powerful, beautiful, and thorough course conveys life-changing lessons in spirituality. In the most loving and inspiring manner, the family group was taught how to pray and meditate, to turn within, ask for help, and learn to grow in unconditional love.

ISBN: 0-931892-54-6,
112 pp., paper, $9.95

Survival Guide for the New Millennium

How to Survive the Coming Earth Changes

Byron Kirkwood

A manual to prepare for and survive the predicted earth changes, containing suggestions and lists of supplies which people should have on hand during and after emergencies.

ISBN: 0-931892-86-4,
144 pp., paper, $11.00

"At times we are given messages in symbols. This book, with its exercises, will help you gain confidence in your ability to receive answers."
—Annie Kirkwood,
Mary's Message to the World

"Mary Jo McCabe is a master at explaining things people have been pondering for decades. She is truly a leader on the forefront of a new evolution of personal growth and development."
—Bonnie Young, CEO,
Creative Renegades, Inc.

Learn to See

An Approach to Your Inner Voice Through Symbols
Mary Jo McCabe with Edwin Greer

From ancient times, the use of symbols has been the key to unlocking a wealth of timeless information into awareness. Learn to reach that quiet place within where true seeing begins, and how to interpret and trust the meanings of images received in dreams and meditation.

Mary Jo provides a conscious approach to everyday life, demonstrating how you can use your personal symbols to open a library of limitless knowledge waiting for you.

"There is a Truth which pulses through the universe, connecting all time and all people. This Truth is available to you if you open yourself to it."

- *proof of our existence after death*
- *convincing, touching, and heartwarming stories of the hereafter*
- *the help we get from spirit at the time of our passing*
- *how our loved ones care for and help us even after they pass over*
- *a peek into the life of a medium*
- *the accuracy (and the humor!) of what spirit can convey through a medium*

ISBN: 0-931892-32-5,
128 pages, $11.00

Through the Eyes of Spirit

Jennifer Christine Crawford

Seeing *Through the Eyes of Spirit*, Jennie Crawford shares her unique perspective as a medium, explaining how spirits communicate through her and why these moments of communication are so precious. She gives us examples of the help, as well as the resolution of deep sadness, that communication with loved ones in spirit provides for many people.

Jenny says, "To me, the true work of a medium is to link these people with their loved ones in the spirit world, to provide them with peace of mind, hope, and encouragement to continue with their lives on the earth plane, knowing that their loved ones in the spirit world have gone on and are safe, well, and happy."

*Do you believe in reincarnation?
Is it fraud? Delusion?
Possession? Genetic memory?
Or . . . could it be . . . that we
have lived before?*

*Best-selling author Brad Steiger
takes us one step closer to
understanding with a startling
new look at reincarnation and
life before life!*

*In researching documented cases
and interviewing well-known
mind explorers, the answer to
one of mankind's greatest
mysteries unfolds:*

ISBN: 0-931892-29-5,
248 pp., 24 photos, $12.95

You Have Lived Before and . . .

You Will Live Again
Dramatic Case Histories of Reincarnation
Brad Steiger

*"In this newly revised and updated edition of his classic
work,* You Will Live Again, *Brad Steiger uses exciting case
histories to show how past lives are influencing the present—
sometimes for the better, sometimes for the worse—but
always for growth. You'll read this book in one sitting!"*
—Dick Sutphen, author of *You Were Born Again to Be Together*

With the vigor of a true explorer, Brad Steiger investigates
fascinating past-life memories and sudden recollections of
places, people, or events not part of this lifetime.

Vol. 1: ISBN: 0-931892-36-8, 160 pp.
Vol. 2: ISBN: 0-931892-37-6, 144 pp.
$12.95/each

Learn about:

- The true infinity of life
- good and evil on earth
- spiritual guides
- wisdom left behind by UFO beings
- why meditation is healing
- the truth behind prayer
- the majesty of life on millions of other planets
- and much, much more

The Teachings of Oscar Camille
Volumes I and II

as given to Paul Edward Napora

"Oscar Camille," an out-of-body guide who lived on earth as a fourth-century monk, discusses the past, present, and future of humanity from the viewpoint of eternity. Messages, predictions, and many other revelations about Earth and Heaven are offered with love, wisdom, purpose, and hope.

In *Volume I,* Oscar Camille answers vital questions about our stay on planet Earth. In *Volume II,* he takes us on a journey to other universes and out-of-body realities. *The Teachings of Oscar Camille* is a vital door meant to be opened.

Open it . . . Read it . . . Embrace it . . . Live it!

"It is possible for every individual to form a personal relationship with the Archangels and receive their loving guidance."

"When you develop an awareness of the presence of angels and invite their participation into your life, magical things begin to happen."

ISBN: 0-931892-25-1, 168 pp., gift/hardcover, $12.95

Inspired by Angels
Letters from the Archangels
Michael, Raphael, Gabriel, & Uriel

Sinda Jordan

Sinda Jordan began receiving messages from the Archangels in 1993. Over the course of a year, the angels dictated many inspiring lessons, which Sinda has compiled into "letters" for everyone to read. Each angel provides loving guidance for specific problems in everyday life and can be called upon for help: Michael, the protector of humanity, for strength; Raphael, the physician of the angelic realm, for healing; Gabriel, for dissolving fear and guiding us through change; Uriel, for emotional and mental clarity.